Elements of Successful TEACHING

General & Special Education Students

Barbara D. Bateman

IEP

RESOURCES

Author: Barbara D. Bateman
Editor: Tom Kinney
Graphic Design: Sherry Pribbenow
Otter Art: Beverly Potts

An Attainment Publication

P.O. Box 930160
Verona, Wisconsin   53593-0160
Phone 800-327-4269   Fax 800.942.3865

www.AttainmentCompany.com

ISBN 1-57861-502-X

Table of Contents

Dedicated to:

Three of the finest teachers ever,
with unbounded admiration for their skills and
deepest gratitude to have known them as friends and as my teachers:

Anita Archer
Annemieke Golly
Marilyn Sprick

Acknowledgments:

Without the daily ups and downs of teaching in the real world of
public secondary schools as I have been privileged to know them
through the lives of my sister Jan and my brother Denny,
I would never have been able to write this book, not in 1972 and not now.
I pray that this book reflects the admiration which I feel for them
and for every teacher who gives, each and every day,
the best that day allows them to give.
We can ask no more. Thank you Puffer and Carrot.

About the Author

Barbara Bateman

Barbara Bateman, Ph.D., J.D. is a nationally
recognized expert in special education and
in special education law. She has taught special
education students in public schools and institutions,
conducted research in learning disabilities, assessment, visual impairments,
mental retardation, attitudes toward people with disabilities, and effective
instruction for children with disabilities. She joined the faculty of the special
education department at the University of Oregon in 1966 and while there
also held visiting or summer appointments at several universities including
the University of Virginia, the University of Maine, and the University of
Wisconsin. She has authored over 100 professional articles, monographs,
chapters and books. Dr. Bateman graduated from the University of Oregon
School of Law in 1976, the year before the federal special education law (then
called P.L. 94-142 and now known as IDEA) went into effect, and since then
has worked in all 50 states, serving as a hearing officer, an expert witness,
a consultant to attorneys and agencies, a speaker, and a teacher of special
education law.

Presently, Dr. Bateman is a special education consultant in private practice.

When not writing, conducting in service education for school districts,
providing assistance to parents of children with disabilities, or consulting
with attorneys involved in IDEA legal actions, Dr. Bateman can be found
traveling the world with binoculars and snorkel in search of birds,
fish and shells.

Forward

This book was first published in 1972 as Essentials of Teaching and was then reprinted in 1992. Now, here it is again, revised to reflect at least two important federal laws that affect everyday classroom activities — The Individuals with Disabilities Act (IDEA) and the recent amendment to the Elementary and Secondary Education Act known as the No Child Left Behind Act of 2001 (NCLB). The first, IDEA, largely affects what teachers do instructionally with the six million school children who have disabilities and are protected by IDEA. The NCLB also affects teachers greatly, in terms of what they teach (more emphasis on academics), how they teach it (methods proven effective in scientific research) and what qualifications they must have as teachers.

Historically, the federal government has not intervened significantly in education. However, in recent decades, it has used its funding power to shape and influence education. The states are offered the "carrot" of federal funding to support federally desired educational programs in exchange for the states' agreement to abide by the regulations which accompany the funding. The Individuals with Disabilities Education Act (IDEA) and the Elementary and Secondary Education Act (including NCLB) operate that way and both represent major change in the ways schools do business. Both entitle students to "qualified" teachers and, arguably, to effective methodology.

This book is about some of the things effective teachers do. At a minimum, our best teachers:

~ create and maintain a positive learning environment in the classroom;

~ have sufficient subject matter knowledge to keep the content of instruction accurate and current;

~ have mastered specific skills of teaching; and

~ maintain high professional standards.

Our focus is briefly on professionalism, then shifts to the skills of teaching per se. Whether teachers are made or born, there are some core teaching skills that can be taught and enhanced. Those are our concern. Our position is that while these skills ought to be mastered by all teachers, they are absolutely crucial for teachers of students who need the best instruction in order to learn effectively. Many of those are students in special education, slow learners, students who are culturally diverse or from economically disadvantaged homes. The teaching practices in this book are good for all students but essential for these.

In the thirty years since the first edition of this book was written, mountains of evidence have accumulated attesting to the validity, efficacy and importance of the teaching principles and practices presented.
One substantive change made in this newest edition is that the original treatment of precision teaching, as developed and advocated by Ogden Lindsley, Eric Haughton, and others, has been shaped into a discussion of the importance of fluency in mastery teaching. Precision teaching involved more than fluency; however, fluency is the portion of the precision teaching legacy which has blossomed and is now in welcome full bloom.

What we occasionally call direct teaching is now well known and respected as "direct instruction," as developed by Siegfried Engelmann and his colleagues over the past four decades. Some specific examples of direct instruction have been deleted from the present edition in favor of recognizing its research-based position of pre-eminence in effective curriculum and methodology.

From today's perspective, thirty years further down the educational road, I still recognize the early influence of Robert Mager, James Popham, Benjamin Bloom and Robert Gagne in my thinking. Now, it is also clear that the greatest formative forces in my professional views were two educational giants — Samuel A. Kirk and Siegfried Engelmann.

I am deeply indebted and grateful to Sam and Zig, but all errors and misjudgments herein belong solely to me.

A.C. Perry, 1912
The Status of the Teacher

*Our teachers will become more and more the masters of
sound pedagogic methods, so that every detail of the
teaching process will be unerringly placed upon
scientific foundations . . .*

*They will become class managers of the highest order,
employing a happy finesse in that most difficult of the school arts,
that which we call discipline . . .*

*Not sufficient as the test of (the teacher's) work will be the questions:
Have his pupils acquired mental acumen?
Can they stand examination in the exercise of logical processes
or the recall of memorized words?*

*Equally applicable will be the tests:
Do his pupils evince human sympathy in ever enlarging degree?
. . . Only when these things are so will the teacher be truly professional.*[1]

1. Perry, A.C. (1912). The Status of the Teacher. Boston, MA: Houghton Mifflin. (p. 64-65)

The Teacher and the Task

Chapter 1

"Real Education"

After a lengthy, bitter, expensive legal battle between school and parents over the education of a student, an observer at the trial said quietly to a companion, "After all this, what really matters, and all that matters, is what happens between that boy and his teachers." What a wise and true perspective. When the laws have been passed or repealed, the budgets passed or failed, the reorganization done and all the memos written, the fact remains that education happens between student and teacher. Teaching is an awesome responsibility. Done well, it is exciting, rewarding and fun, as well as hard work.

Whether students or teachers are identified as "general" or "special" education, the core principles of professionalism and of effective teaching are the same. Human beings learn as we learn, but some learn more readily than others. Some need nearly perfect teaching; others learn in spite of much that is imperfect. Our view is that everything truly said about good teaching is important for all teachers, regular and special education, alike. Sometimes focusing on special education can help us see general education more clearly, as if through a magnifying glass.

Ozzie's Words of Wisdom

Whether students or teachers are identified as "general" or "special" education, the core principles of professionalism and of effective teaching are the same.

Ozzie the Otter

Special education is now defined in the Individuals with Disabilities Education Act (IDEA) regulations as "specially designed instruction to meet the unique needs of the child." Most, if not all special education students, need superb instruction while many regular education students seem to learn readily by osmosis, by just being alive in the world. By definition, to be IDEA eligible, a student must need special education, i.e., specially designed instruction, and exceptional execution of that instruction.

Historically, special education had a nurturing and protective element. By the 1960s that emphasis had largely been replaced by a focus on careful, intensive instruction.

Zigmond, speaking for many of us, especially in the fields of learning disabilities and behavior disorders, recalls:

". . . how optimistic we were about the outcomes for students who received properly implemented special education. It "fixed" them. It taught them things they had not learned before, despite opportunities to learn in the mainstream or in the community. Special education taught what could not be learned anywhere else.

"In addition, the special education teacher was uniquely prepared for the task. She had learned how to figure out what each individual student assigned to her needed to know and how to teach it. Sometimes she just asked; sometimes she observed; sometimes she tested. Then she designed instructional activities, made materials, and taught. The special educator was detective and diagnostician. She was clever and creative. She knew a lot about children and about instruction, and she knew that students were depending on her to help them achieve. Above all else, however, she was relentless. She did not give up until she and her students had been successful . . . The (special education) teachers who left teacher preparation programs in those early years had a mission . . . They were prepared to teach intensively, preferably one-to-one."[1]

However, by the mid-1980s, the special education scene had changed until it was hardly recognizable. Teachers had case loads of 50, 75, or 100 students, dozens of IEP meetings plus other IDEA paperwork, collaboration and consultation duties and on and on. The results of this reduced ability to teach were predictable – special education students learned less and less. By the time IDEA was amended by Congress in 1997, the situation was dire. Therefore, IDEA was refocused on student progress, on the measurable and measured results of teaching, on the actual outcomes of special education. An exclamation point was added to this "emphasis on achievement" when just a few years later the No Child Left Behind Act (NCLB) was passed with requirements for increasing the numbers of "highly qualified" teachers in our classrooms; the objective assessing of all students' academic progress (except for less than 1% who

Ozzie's Words of Wisdom

By the mid-1980s, the special education scene had changed until it was hardly recognizable. Teachers had case loads of 50, 75, or 100 students, dozens of IEP meetings plus other IDEA paperwork, collaboration and consultation duties, and on and on.

The results of this reduced ability to teach were predictable.

have severe or profound cognitive disabilities); and requiring schools to meet Adequate Yearly Progress (AYP) goals.

Welcome forces, including IDEA and NCLB, are now coalescing to compel us to look more closely once again at effective teaching and how to bring it about.

Ozzie's Words of Wisdom

Over the last twenty years it has become fashionable to pretend that special education students learn at much the same rate as other students, and that they're receiving the intensive teaching that allow them to learn more in a shorter period of time and thus catch up. Both premises are flawed.

Most special education students demonstrate well before their first referral, that they don't learn as readily as do others from the typical loosely structured educational environment. To the contrary, they need as nearly perfect teaching as can be provided.

This book spells out some best teaching practices. Every student would benefit from them, but for special education students they are critical. It is a truism that when a teaching practice is effective for special education students — as are those in this book — they will also be effective for regular education students. The converse is not always true.

Engelmann has powerfully explicated the essential role of mastery teaching for low performers (many of whom are or may become special education students):

". . . acceleration of intellectual performance in any subject is possible by teaching to mastery. This type of acceleration is rarely observed in traditional educational settings, however, because lower performers rarely master material when it is taught and, therefore, have a poorly developed and inefficient mental schema for learning to mastery (e.g., poor memory, large number of trials required to induce mastery,

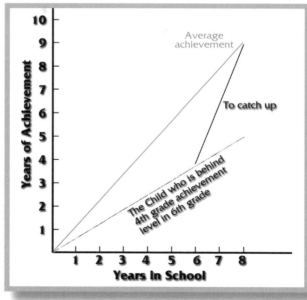

*We must teach more **intensively** if a child is to catch up.*

tendencies to mislearn, low tolerance for failure, low level of motivation).

"Often, attempts to help lower performers do not provide help. For example, "inclusive" practices that place the child in the same classroom as the average performer are supposed to make the lower performers feel good about themselves because they are not stigmatized by being in the special classroom. The assumption of these practices is that somehow the lower performer will be able to perform better in this setting and will be able to keep pace with the others. A logical analysis of what is required for the lower performer to do this, however, shows how preposterous the practice is. The basic problem is that the amount of new learning required for the lower performer to achieve mastery in this setting is significantly greater than this learner can achieve."[2]

Over the last twenty years or so it has become fashionable to pretend either that special education students learn at much at the same rate as do other students and that they are receiving the superb, intensive teaching that will allow them to learn more in a shorter period of time and thus catch up. Both premises are flawed.

However, now IDEA and NCLB, as well as professional integrity, require that we begin today to offer the best teaching we can to all students and especially to those protected by IDEA – the six million in special education. The President's Commission on Excellence in Special Education has stated that NCLB must now become the driving force behind IDEA. What does it require?

Ozzie's Words of Wisdom

Seldom, if ever, have so many been so dissatisfied with the job being done by the schools. Every facet of education from books to budgets and tests to teachers has been found wanting.

NCLB primary educational reforms include:

~ an increased accountability for all students reaching proficiency in academics by 2013-2014,

~ greater parental choice when schools remain low performing,

~ a utilization of scientific, research-based, proven-effective instructional methods and professional development programs, and

~ all students taught by highly qualified teachers by 2005-2006.

One intent of the lawmakers clearly is to increase teacher effectiveness, i.e., to enable teachers to cause greater student learning. But how do teachers induce learning?

Suppose tryouts, auditions or contests were held for teachers, as they sometimes are for actors, musicians, dancers, or athletes who wish to perform in a particular capacity. What would we ask aspiring teachers to do to demonstrate competence in teaching? Clearly little consensus exists as to all the specific skills teachers need and the priority assigned to each. But perhaps a core of essential teaching skills can be identified to which all would agree.

In a well attended public debate, a prominent professor of education lashed out at a colleague who authored a highly structured and successful reading program, declaring, "After all, the Nazis taught kids to read! What does that have to do with real education?" While its emotionalism might have been toned down some, the remark was a vivid reminder that there may be more to educating children than just inculcating specific skills. Teaching students to read, write and count are a vital, worthwhile, and paramount task of education, and how a child feels about his own abilities is also important. Further, the purposes to which the student later applies skills are important and are at least partially the responsibility of the educative process.

Our schools have indeed been given a tall order — to educate children in a manner that pleases everyone, with results we all can applaud while doing it at a cost we can afford. Hardly a walk in the park.

The Purpose of Education – Why Do We Teach?

Ozzie's Words of Wisdom

It is a truism that when a teaching practice is effective for special education students — as are those in this book — they will also be effective for regular education students. The converse is not always true.

Current criticism of our schools, including special and general education, ranges from mild to bombastic. A noted journalist sadly observed that in his 57 years of reporting on the American scene, public education has gotten steadily worse and has hit rock bottom. Our high school students score in math and science in the bottom 10% of developed nations, and our graduation rates are 17th even when improving our education system has been a top priority of our last five presidents.[3]

Seldom, if ever, have so many been so dissatisfied with the job being done by the schools. Every facet of education from books to budgets and tests to teachers has been found wanting. At least two problems emerge from these analyses:

~ the objectives of education are unclear, and

~ many children have not learned as much or as well as we believe they should have. Congress, through the NCLB, is now attempting to bring about a federal fix to both of these problems.

Ozzie's Words of Wisdom

The humanitarian goals and values of educators can most effectively be reached by precise, systematic and scientific procedures.

A growing number of concerned educators believe that until schools at every level have precisely defined statements of what they are attempting to do, the likelihood of doing it remains small. Vague, global intentions such as "fostering good citizenship" seemed adequate enough in years past and went largely unchallenged. During World War II, most of us knew that a "good citizen" supported the war effort and cheated only rarely with gasoline or sugar stamps. However, events since then have made us realize our nation is no longer of one mind about how the "good citizen" conducts himself in relation to our government.

Most of us want the schools to produce young citizens who are cognitively and academically competent, and who are concerned, caring humanitarians eager to build a better world than the one we have passed on to them. Some educators have concerns with affective issues like self-esteem, yet they are not necessarily in conflict with the behaviorally oriented educators who advocate precise objectives and systematic interventions followed by empirical evaluation. The humanitarian goals and values of educators can most effectively be reached by precise, systematic and scientific procedures. Teaching a child to be an independent problem solver can best be accomplished by the careful and precise kinds of procedures presented in this book. One key to the use of scientific procedures to achieve affective ends is to specify clearly what we're hoping to achieve. NCLB requires that states define "adequate yearly progress" objectively, using standardized achievement test scores. This is a start.

Thousands of thick volumes have been devoted to the philosophy of education and the role of schools in our society. The issues are complex and changing, no doubt. However, many believe that until educators clearly articulate measurable objectives, chaos will continue to reign. Precisely defined educational objectives sometimes seem too narrow to include all the aspirations held for education. But that is no reason to avoid them. If a certain elementary school has become notorious for producing academically low-achieving youngsters, a specific objective to adopt could be "increasing average student achievement test scores by six months." While that would not be a complete statement about what the school was trying to do, it is a real and measurable objective. Our inability to define all objectives behaviorally should not deter us from formulating those we can.

IDEA has required measurable goals, benchmarks and objectives on every special education student's IEP since 1977. Even so, writing them has not yet become second nature to most IEP developers. But when they are well done, they form the basis for assessing progress. Without measurable objectives and goals, we are just guessing whether we have reached them. As important as measurable objectives are for all educators and students, they are indispensable for special education teachers and students.

In the next chapter we deal more extensively with instructional objectives for students. It should also be noted that teachers should set instructional goals for themselves, too. For example, a first grade teacher might recognize that a third of her students were going into second grade unable to correctly respond to the short vowels. She might determine to reduce that number by half. By no means is that all she would attempt to achieve that year, but it's a start.

> ### Ozzie's Words of Wisdom
>
> *As important as measurable objectives are for all educators and students, they are indispensable for special education teachers and students.*

With NCLB we now have, at a national level, annual objective assessments required in reading and math for grades 3 – 8, annual school report cards and mandated annual measurable objectives to measure student progress. More than thirty years ago, when this book was originally written, it was well known and accepted by data-based educators that objectives were essential. Even so, widespread use of specific objectives was not in sight. Now, we have a federal mandate requesting states that want federal funding to publicly put forth and meet objective, academic progress criteria for all students. Who said we don't ever make progress in education? However, the most interesting question will be answered in 35 years — will measurable objectives and goals still be required, still used, still taught? Or will they give way to education's 35 year cycle?

Our view is that until we are able and willing to state our educational intentions (at least some of them) so clearly that the community knows what they are and can readily judge whether they were achieved, we are going to flounder, fizzle and worse.

Professionalism

Over thirty years ago, a group of educators attempted to envision teaching as it would be a decade later. Their analysis yielded five major clusters of behaviors. Their judgment was that teachers, a decade later, would have to be able to:

1. Formulate objectives in terms of observable and measurable behavior.

2. Select and organize content consistently with the logic of the content and with the psychological demands of the learner.

3. Employ appropriate strategies for the attainment of desired behavioral objectives.

4. Evaluate instructional outcomes in terms of behavioral changes.

5. Demonstrate competence and willingness to accept professional responsibilities and serve as a professional leader.[4]

The last essential behavior above — accepting professional responsibilities — is clearly of a different order than the first four and more difficult to translate into specific behaviors.

The remainder of this book will deal with the first four essentials of teaching — selecting objectives, organizing content, teaching and evaluating. These essentials of teaching (plus one) we call OTTER teaching:

Objectives (instructional goals)

Task Analysis (organizing content)

Teaching (content)

Evaluating (results of teaching)

Recycling (teach again)
    or Rejoicing (enjoy your success)

OTTER teaching is easily recalled by "Hey, we really OTTER wanna' teach like this!"

Before we plunge directly into OTTER teaching, we need to look briefly at that important, but elusive "other" dimension of teaching — professionalism. How can we tell a more professional teacher from a less professional one? What are teacher behaviors we describe as professional?

1. The Professional Teacher can Articulate a Personal Philosophy of Education

We're not saying all teachers should share similar views of the purpose of school, but that each should have a clear ordering of priorities as the basis for decision-making in the classroom. After all, if we fail to revive interest in questioning what schools are for, we may find them vanishing.
The professional teacher must have a belief in the role of the school in society and be familiar with the philosophical positions which emphasize its diverse functions, such as fostering social or vocational adjustment.
And she's aware of the "left-over rule," which holds that the school is uniquely suited to pick up training functions, such as sex education, as they are dropped by other societal agencies or institutions.

Ozzie's Words of Wisdom

Today's teachers know all too well the "left-over rule," which holds that the school is uniquely suited to pick up training functions, such as sex education, as they are dropped by other societal agencies or institutions.

A professional teacher will ask many difficult questions. Those who believe schools should prepare children for self-government may find it difficult to justify an administration-imposed dress code. If a school district could afford new uniforms for the football team or a new, research-based reading program, which would your staff choose and what does it say about the purpose of the school? Does your staff feel that the primary job of the school is to teach all children to read and write? That until the school does a better job of teaching basic skills, it has no business taking on other tasks? Do the economic realities of our times require that schools be inefficient, i.e., teach literacy skills slowly, not very well, and not to all children? Is it true that if we taught as well as our technology and science allow us, we would have too many well-educated persons in the job market refusing to accept low-wage jobs? (This is not a radical jibe, but a position proposed in a respected education newsletter.) What does your philosophy of education say about the pre-school movement which advocates systematic teaching of skills and cognitive strategies to maximize chances of academic success in first grade and later years? Should schools be run, as some suggest, for children? The notion of the teacher as an advocate for students is often being expressed these days. A five-year-old boy who reads comfortably at a fourth-grade level visited the school where he was to enroll as a first-grader in the fall. His first wish was to see the library, since he had exhausted the resources of his tiny previous one. When this eager fellow found the library in his new school, he was immediately told that "First graders are not allowed to use this library. Your teacher will get all your books for you." Should schools be run for children, even when it means administrative inconveniences?

Special education teachers have an even more complicated task in thinking through their role today. They must deal with the bedeviling issue of justifying higher taxpayer expenditures for lower performance results. It may be observed that a society can be judged by how it treats those least able to fend for themselves.

In times apparently long gone, special education teachers had to be able to defend their smaller case loads, slightly higher salaries and their independence as they travelled from building to building. Now the inevitable question is "How do you justify the advantages given to students in special education over others (an IEP, a Free Appropriate Public Education, due process)? Difficult questions, indeed.

2. The Professional Teacher is Willing to be an Agent of Social Change

More than three decades ago, Goodlad listed some of the most frequently discussed educational practices which one might expect to someday see in our schools. How many of these are now fully in place 35 years later?

1. Efforts to determine where the student is at the beginning of instruction, to diagnose his attainments and problems, and to base instruction on the diagnosis.

2. Learning directed toward self-sustaining inquiry rather than memorization and regurgitation of facts.

3. Students involved in direct observation of physical and human phenomena.

4. Classrooms containing a wide variety of learning materials — records, tapes, programmed materials — not dominated by textbooks.

5. Concern for individual differences in assignments, class discussions, use of materials, grouping practices and evaluation.

6. Teachers using learning principles such as reinforcement, motivation and transfer of training.

7. Use of vigorous group discussions with the teacher assuming a background role.

8. Flexible school environments marked by little attention to grade levels, extensive use of team teaching.

9. Innovative handling of special educational problems such as those presented by environmentally handicapped children.[5]

The fact is that these educational practices, recommended thirty years ago, are not currently implemented as widely as they should be. What are teachers doing to insure immediate and increased use of these and related techniques?

Most of us view teaching as a commitment to do our best to teach certain things to those in our tutelage. There are some factors teachers can't affect, but must be taken into account. Among these are: The number of children in the classroom; amount of money available for purchasing educational materials; length of the school day and year; nature of learning materials available; school regulations pertaining to out-of-school activities such as field trips. Most teachers argue that many of these factors are not under their control, even though they can substantially affect the instructional process. Teachers sometimes sum up their frustrations by saying, "I have to close my door and do the best I can with what I have to work with." Unfortunately, the plain and simple truth is never plain and simple. On the one hand, such dedication to doing the best you can within real world limitations is commendable. Conversely, there is a danger of accepting some limitations as givens, when in fact they could be modified.

Ozzie's Words of Wisdom

Professionalism includes a willingness to be accountable for the results of our teaching efforts, to objectively and clearly demonstrate them and to change our practices when we must.

In past years, research studies have characterized teachers as being conservative regarding social action to effect change (there are many exceptions). Historical reasons for this timidity abound. But this is one area where times have changed. Most teachers now have some protection from overt silencing, if not from subtle pressures. But, protection is not the issue. Is it possible that a commitment to teaching requires us to assume a more active role in change? Just for discussion, assume that the superiority of reading program A has been amply demonstrated, as measured by student reading performance. Does the teacher who is aware of this fact have a professional obligation to work for the purchase of this program? Move one step further from the classroom and suppose the teacher knows the nutritional deficiencies suffered by a student hinder his learning. Does the teacher have a professional obligation to act? What if she has conscientiously referred this student to school or public health officials and the deficiency has been confirmed, but not alleviated? Does this end the teacher's responsibility? Can the educator who is committed to teaching always distinguish between her instructional role and that of concerned citizen? What if the teacher in Room 101 frequently overhears her counterpart in Room 102 behaving in a discriminatory way toward certain children? Too many special education teachers are confronted daily by district or building practices they know to be in violation of IDEA. How far does the prudent teacher go in advocating for a child? These questions have no easy answers. The teacher's job is to ponder them and to work within professional parameters to bring about necessary change.

3. The Professional Teacher is Accountable

Perhaps the word "accountable" is used too easily. What should it mean to the teacher? It includes being data-based, accepting responsibility for the results of teaching and being willing to change. The accountable classroom teacher is eager to share with colleagues and community precise and full data on the academic performances of her students. This includes reporting objectives, and data on how many reached which objective. Wouldn't it be reassuring if, as parents, we could call a prospective reading teacher of

Ozzie's Words of Wisdom

Is it possible that a commitment to teaching children requires the teacher of today to assume a more active role in change?

our child and be told, "In seven years of teaching first grade, I have had 200 children, and 193 of them scored at least two months above grade level. Of the remaining seven, three read at grade level, two read one month below grade level and one failed." Or what if she said, "This is my first year teaching third grade and of 24 children, 22 read in the third grade book or higher at a minimum rate of 95 words correct per minute. The other two entered my room reading at primer level with 25 words correct per minute." The accountable teacher supports and urges the use of such data. To disallow the public to know how effectively schools teach reading is itself unprofessional. The No Child Left Behind Act will make some of the measured outcomes of education more accessible to communities.

Ozzie's Words of Wisdom

We learn many things without having been taught, and not all that is "taught" is learned.

A related aspect of professionalism is that teachers accept responsibility for their outcomes. Accepting responsibility requires that we distinguish between teaching and learning. People and their behaviors continually change. Not all observable changes are due to learning, however. Some are caused by growth or maturation, some by fatigue, some by pathology. All demonstrated learning involves behavioral change, but not all behavioral change is the result of learning. Similarly, we learn many things without having been taught, and not all that is taught is learned. Our attempts to teach do not always succeed. When no learning occurs, or the learner learns something other than what we are attempting to teach, we can't say we have taught successfully. To sum up: Some changes in our behavior are due to learning, but not all; some learning is due to teaching, but not all.

Teaching implies that we arrange something so learning occurs. One is tempted to use "deliberate" in describing our teaching efforts, but this could mislead since we can inadvertently teach very different things than we intend. We might teach children to have temper tantrums by arranging the environment so they are reinforced even when we try to stop them. We sometimes teach children such unfortunate concepts as "I can't do school work," when we are trying to teach the opposite. It is often our arrangement of the environment, rather than our intentions, that determines what we teach. Incidental learning is a term frequently used to describe learning that goes on when the environment hasn't been specifically arranged for it to occur. Most gifted children excel in incidental learning. Parents sometimes report that their gifted child learned to read by himself — no one taught him.

The environment (TV commercials, newspapers, traffic signs, cereal boxes) taught him incidentally, not deliberately.

In this book, teaching refers to intentional arranging or manipulating of the environment so the child will learn more efficiently than if she were to learn incidentally. We will also discuss times when our lack of precision in arranging the environment results in the child learning something other than what we intended.

Teachers sometimes have difficulty viewing themselves as controllers or manipulators of the environment. It all sounds a bit cold or mechanical and doesn't seem to give credit to other roles they fulfill, such as providing an atmosphere in which the student is free to explore or play without being required to learn specific new behaviors. Teachers do perform functions other than careful and precise teaching of specific concepts or skills, especially with young children. But those functions might best be described as something other than teaching. Perhaps they could be called nurturing, or supervisory. Teachers do things other than teach; but our major concern is with instructional functions.

If the teacher makes a presentation and the children are then able to perform as she intended, has she taught them? Not necessarily. Children often learn what the teacher hopes they will learn but learn it somewhere else. A teaching presentation may be inadequate and yet children appear to learn from it. The fact that children do learn even when teaching is inadequate makes it difficult to evaluate the instruction. Engelmann has expressed this point with specific reference to teaching children to read:

> "The authors of reading programs have typically approached in an awkward way the problem of teaching children to read. They have worked with average children of about six and one-half years. These children are relatively sophisticated. They have a pretty good idea of what reading is and they know what they are supposed to do in a new learning situation. They know how to treat words as sounds and not merely as signals that convey content. They play word games; they rhyme and alliterate. They probably know letter names and have a fair idea of some letter sounds. These children are able to learn to read from a variety of approaches, so they are thus able to compensate for gaps in an instructional program. They often learn in spite of the program. If the program does not provide adequate instruction for a particular subskill such as rhyming or blending, the children usually learn anyhow.

"The author . . . cannot clearly see the relationship between the effectiveness of his program and the children's reading performance. He cannot clearly see which skills he has successfully taught, which skills were taught before the child began the program, and which were obliquely induced through instruction . . . Typically, he presumes that he is responsible for a great deal more than he deserves credit for . . . If the children succeed, the program is responsible; if they fail, the children are responsible. The instruction is exonerated from all responsibility for failure. Obviously, this situation is not healthy and does not promote better instruction."[6]

A major focus of our discussion will be on developing an approach to teaching which increases our ability to be responsible for its outcomes. We need to learn how to actively cause the desired learning rather than hoping that a potpourri of prior or incidental learning and happy circumstances will coalesce in our favor.

The accountable professional teacher is willing to change — to learn or in some cases, to unlearn — when a practice is shown to be in the child's best interests.

It can be difficult to say, "I used to teach only the names of letters to my kindergartners, but now I know it's better to also teach sounds." Is it difficult because we never really thought about it and just did what was customary? Perhaps we have never experienced the praise that thinking people give to one who has re-evaluated and changed a position. Whatever the reasons for past failures to go where data, logic, evidence and common sense take us, the professional teacher must make decisions about what is in the child's best interest on rational grounds.

Ozzie's Words of Wisdom

If the child's program was not monitored, or was monitored but no corrective action taken, it's possible the child has been denied a free appropriate public education.

Special education teachers sometimes fear the consequences when students fail to accomplish the goals and objectives of IEPs. In fact, such shortcomings are not, by themselves, the basis for legal action. However, if the child's program was not monitored, or was monitored but no corrective action taken, then it's possible the student has been denied a free appropriate public education.

Until NCLB imposed accountability for student progress on Title I schools, IDEA was the only federal law holding schools accountable for inadequate educational services. History may well write that the 21st century ushered legal accountability onto the U.S. education scene.

4. The Professional Teacher has Certain Knowledge and Specific Competencies

A current approach to improving skills of new teachers is to establish behavioral objectives for teacher training programs. The procedures of developing such skills-oriented curricula are essentially the same that we advocate classroom teachers use in planning instruction within their rooms:

~ The educational objective is stated behaviorally. For example, teacher-trainees will administer positive consequences to change student behaviors.

~ A performance criterion must be developed stating how well the trainee must perform each objective. For example, the student whose behavior is being changed by the trainee must manifest a ten-fold change in rate of behavior, i.e., if the pupil was able to perform single column addition problems correctly at a rate of 2 per minute, the teacher must use positive consequences to bring about a rate of 20 per minute; if the pupil was talking-out without permission 5 times an hour, the trainee must reduce the rate to .5 per hour; if the pupil was initiating positive verbal interaction with peers only 1 time per recess, the teacher must increase that rate to 10 times.

~ Plan a variety of instructional tactics by which the teacher-trainee could develop the specified competencies. Ideally, several routes are available to achieve any given competency and the learner has appreciable latitude in choosing a route. If a trainee enters the program already able to perform a skill, she is given an opportunity to demonstrate competence and no further instruction is required.

~ Delineate acceptable competency demonstrations for all objectives and procedures to evaluate the effectiveness of instructional tactics.

Ozzie's Words of Wisdom

Until NCLB imposed accountability for student progress on Title I schools, IDEA was the only federal law holding schools accountable for inadequate educational services. History may well write that the 21st century ushered legal accountability onto the U.S. education scene.

The educational objectives for a teacher education program should include actual classroom skills such as:

~ designing instructional situations (writing a task analysis for reaching desired student performances and constructing an instructional sequence);

~ selecting and developing materials (naming and developing materials for a given objective);

~ assessing pupil performance (recording behavior change, evaluating behavior recording systems, assessing student learning aptitude on a variety of dimensions);

~ managing consequences for learning (describing reinforcement systems, assessing student reinforcement preferences, using reinforcers to change and maintain behaviors);

~ orchestrating the classroom (organizing the environment to facilitate management and teaching, managing student behavior);

~ teaching directly (gaining pupil attention, presenting concepts unambiguously, eliciting responses from each student, reinforcing and/or correcting student responses); and

~ taking advantage of spontaneous learning situations.

One teacher training program's efforts to operationalize teaching behaviors resulted in the identification of more than 2,000 specific and essential teacher behaviors. While we support this movement toward accountability on the part of teacher education programs, we cannot deal with each of 2,000 or more specific behaviors every teacher needs. Instead we will use these clusters of essential teacher skills:

~ Writing educational objectives behaviorally so that the extent to which they are accomplished can be assessed.

~ Describing educational tasks so that it's possible to pinpoint student behavior in terms of which relevant subskills have been learned and which still need to be taught.

> ## Ozzie's Words of Wisdom
>
> *Can we roll back the years before our defenses were high and once again feel the joy of an adult telling us we did a really good job? . . . Or, conversely, recall the blinding, choking frustration of being falsely accused and knowing we couldn't explain the truth?*

~ Intervening with effective education procedures which result in efficient learning and positive attitudes toward the process.

~ Evaluating the teaching process so necessary changes can be made.

~ Creating a humane, caring environment for all. She believes in the nurturance of valued traits. One's philosophy of education and beliefs about human nature determine which traits will be especially nurtured. Sometimes in our eagerness to respect the potential of a student, we inadvertently deny the validity of who he is. How do we demonstrate our present valuing of a child? How do we show we really care? The Golden Rule sums it up well, but living by it with 27 children at one time requires that we remember certain feelings, joys and fears. Can we roll back the years before our defenses were high and once again feel the joy of an adult telling us we did a really good job? . . . The blinding frustration of being falsely accused and knowing we couldn't explain the truth? . . .
The urgency of finishing that page of arithmetic problems even if it was time for music? . . . The warm glow of sharing a secret with an adult who was really our friend?. . . The stomach gripping panic that we would be the last one chosen for the team? . . . The heavy, flat nothing when we were so eager to share our excitement about the new puppies and were told to "Take your seat, we don't have time for that now?" . . . Hating gym day because our socks were more hole than sock?

Many workshops are offered where teachers can "learn to listen to children." Some teachers don't need to learn; it's as if they've always known. Others do need to learn, and there are techniques for teaching us to really listen. Professional teachers may sometimes fail to reach a child, but they never put a child down. There is a world of difference, made up of respect and trust, and caring and sheer fun.

Ozzie's Words of Wisdom

Many workshops are offered where teachers can "learn to listen to children." Some teachers don't need to learn; it's as if they've always known. Others do, and there are techniques for teaching them to really listen.

Summary

1. Education consists of direct teaching and self-instruction and is concerned with affective and cognitive domains.

2. Essential teaching behaviors include:

   ~ Writing behavioral instructional objectives.

   ~ Describing, sequencing, and planning instructional strategies for educational tasks.

   ~ Intervening to bring about effective learning.

   ~ Evaluating the efficacy of instruction.

   ~ Accepting professional responsibility and leadership.

3. The professional teacher was described as one who has a philosophy of education, who is willing to be an agent of change on behalf of children, who is accountable, who possesses a high degree of specific skills and knowledge related to teaching, and who "cares."

4. The accountable teacher is one who makes data-based educational decisions and shares data about student performance, distinguishes between learning and teaching, accepts responsibility for the outcomes and is willing to change, to learn new behaviors and unlearn old ones.

Instructional Objectives

Chapter II

A growing number of educators and non-educators believe that substantial and essential improvement in instruction cannot happen until we all use behavioral objectives. We believe, with them, that using behavioral objectives is a vital step each teacher must take to substantially improve teaching. Without behaviorally stated instructional objectives, it remains forever impossible to evaluate how well we have accomplished our intentions. If the readers of this book become measurably more precise and exact in their own formulations of what they are attempting to teach, our efforts will have been amply rewarded. The first step toward better teaching will have been taken. And a giant step it is.

Many of us can recall the excitement of graduating from the "tadpole" swimming class to the "salamanders" to the "trout" and finally to the "sharks." Perhaps we can even remember some of the performances required — to face float unsupported for five seconds or swim 100 yards using three different strokes. The swimming instructor and the student knew precisely what was being taught and how to tell when it was accomplished. In this chapter teachers learn to formulate educational objectives with the same clarity and utility. The focus of swimming objectives was on what the learner could do as a result of instruction, and so it will be on learner outcomes. Teachers should also prepare objectives which refer to their own behavior, e.g., "Return each pupil paper, with comments, no more than 24 hours after the paper was submitted."

Ozzie's Words of Wisdom

" . . . I am thoroughly committed, both rationally and viscerally to the proposition that instructional goals should be stated behaviorally . . . those who discourage educators from precisely explicating their instructional objectives are often permitting, if not promoting, the same kind of unclear thinking that has led in part to the generally abysmal quality of instruction in this country."

(Popham, 1969)[1]

The need for specific and precise instructional objectives is obvious — or is it? Many have noted that if we don't know where we're going we might end up someplace else. To complicate matters even more, if we don't know where we're going, we can't determine when we've arrived!

The casual treatment of objectives in some educational circles is difficult to appreciate. A curriculum guide on the writer's desk lists the six "Objectives of Education" for a particular school system as "Citizenship, Family Life, Moral and Spiritual Values, Basic Skills of Communication, Health and Esthetic Expression and Economic Life." As objectives, these are useless. They give no indication of what to teach, how to teach it, or how to know when you have taught it. They also provide almost no information about what not to teach. It's difficult to conceive of a single human endeavor which couldn't be placed under one or more of these headings. Objectives which tell us neither what to teach nor what not to teach are hardly helpful.

Objective: Appreciate Multiplicative Relationships

If an objective of education is to be of any value, it must be attainable. That is to say, we must be able to determine whether an objective has been reached. An attainable educational objective would be to "Teach all the children in the room to orally recite multiplication tables without error." It would be fairly simple to determine when this objective had been reached. In contrast, "to fully develop the concept of multiplicative relationships" would not be useful as an objective, since it needs more specification. Throughout this discussion of objectives we are speaking not of broad designations but about specific statements of what students will be able to do as a result of instruction.

Objective: Recite Multiplication Tables

Selection of Objectives

No teacher can teach everything to all students in her charge. Attention must be given to selecting the most important educational objectives. But, important to whom and by what standards of importance? We have less than total agreement about what constitutes appropriate educational objectives. This may relate to a desire to be all-inclusive, but while the concept of the "well-rounded" program is appealing, our attempts to do a little bit of everything for everyone has resulted in an inadequate job of teaching much of anything to anyone. The crescendo of dissatisfaction with the reading achievement of today's students is just one indication that we are not doing the primary instructional job the public feels is our responsibility.

If we stop for a moment and calculate the portion of time a child is in school, the need for selectivity and the impossibility of doing all things for all students becomes apparent. There are 8,760 hours in a year, and based on a generous five-hour instructional day, a child is in school 900 hours per year. Therefore, less than 11% of a year (less than 20% of a child's waking time) is spent in school. A recent study found the average amount of instructional time in one elementary school was $1^1/_2$ hours per day. This figure yields 3% of a student's total time available to the teacher for instructional purposes. Add to these figures today's knowledge explosion and we realize there is so much to teach and so little time in which to teach it, that we must be highly selective. This doesn't mean we don't want to teach everything to everybody; it means we cannot do it. Therefore, we must limit ourselves to the most important content, skills and experiences which are the school's responsibility (rather than that of some other societal institution).

Criteria for Selection

The responsibility for choosing, from the entire range of knowledge, what to teach is humbling, and teachers are increasingly assuming their professional role in developing, arguing for, and implementing an educational philosophy. Regardless of tradition, curriculum guides, or other restraints, they are emphasizing problem-solving, decision-making, self-esteem and social responsibility.

The amount of help available from existing curriculum guides and textbooks is variable. Supposing certain topics (topics, not objectives) are "givens." The curriculum guide requires, for example, that sixth graders are to study the geography and resources of South America. The teacher's concern then begins with what exactly is to be learned by the children. How is the teacher to use the unit on South America to increase problem-solving and decision-making capacities? The inescapable fact is that by omission or commission these decisions are the teacher's and will affect what the sixth graders learn about South America and about themselves as learners. One guideline often used by teachers is to see what the textbook authors and editors have chosen to include in the questions at the end of each section. While it is by no means a poor guide,

Ozzie's Words of Wisdom

There is so much to teach and so little time in which to teach it, that we must be highly selective. Therefore, we must limit ourselves to the most important content, skills, and experiences which are the school's responsibility.

it's not the best guide either. The text does not always provide specific objectives. Remember that a topic, an area, or a focus is not the same as an objective.

As a starting point in selecting objectives, remember that students aren't likely to recall a very high percentage of the particular bits of information to which they are exposed. Supposing there were only ten things the student would remember two years after the unit on South America. What ten things would the teacher want those to be?
Two helpful guides are:

~ what information (data, process, or affective experience) will be the most useful in terms of further learning about related topics and

~ what are the concepts students should have about the resources and geography of any area?

Student Selection of Objectives

So far we have discussed the importance of writing objectives behaviorally. The emphasis is placed here because it's the teacher's professional job to have clearly stated objectives, but it's not entirely the teacher's responsibility. One major purpose of education is to assist students in becoming more proficient at establishing and pursuing their own goals and objectives. Young children can be taught a degree of genuine responsibility for decision-making and selection of activities of value to them. As "experts" on child raising have pointed out, a three year old may not be able to make a wise decision about whether he wants fruit juice, but he is capable of deciding whether he wants orange or tomato juice. When he has made this decision, the responsibility for drinking it is more real than if he had been given no choice. Similarly, a first grader may not have the experience necessary to make an intelligent decision about whether he wants to learn addition before or after subtraction, but he may be able to make decisions about the kind of addition practice he prefers. The teacher's role becomes one of providing a range of alternatives and information about consequences for choices the child might make. The phrase "freedom within limits" may be trite from overuse, but it is still an accurate way of describing how the teacher must provide genuine decision-making and responsibility-taking skills. At the same time there are some non-negotiable "givens" within any social group, including a classroom. If all children were taught to assume increasingly larger pieces of responsibility for their own education beginning with kindergarten, then by upper elementary school age they could cooperatively establish their own rules. But decision-making, initiative-taking, self-evaluation, self-discipline, and so on must be as carefully taught and reinforced as long division or spelling. The ultimate responsibility for having objectives formulated and increasing student decision-making and problem-solving skills is still the teacher's.

General Guidelines for Including Students in Setting Objectives Include:

1. The teacher should immediately give students as large a role as they can assume in formulating their own educational objectives, developing strategies for teaching those objectives and evaluating their efforts.

2. The teacher should continually teach students to assume an ever-increasing amount of responsibility for their own educational decision-making.

3. The teacher should provide a range of alternatives from which the students can select. The objectives themselves are often less negotiable than the means for reaching the objectives.

4. The teacher should assume that students are capable of initiating, and implementing and evaluating worthwhile educational experiences.

The evidence that teachers need to do more to involve students in educating themselves is nowhere more vivid than at the university level. Here we find many students immobilized when the instructor asks them to establish individual course objectives. Often, if pushed about their reluctance to develop their own goals, they acknowledge they have no reason for taking the course except that it is available or required. Only a few undergraduate college students believe they have any right, let alone responsibility, to approach a subject area in terms of what they would like to be able to do, think about or explore. It's as if somehow along the way they have become disassociated from their own education. The education seems to exist "out there" in books or in instructors and is to be pasted onto the student. This is a far cry from our idealized notion of active education happening between the student and his world.

Selecting Objectives – An Illustration

Gronlund suggests five questions which will help teachers select and evaluate their objectives:

~ Do the objectives indicate learning outcomes appropriate to the instructional area?

~ Do the objectives represent all logical learning outcomes of the instructional area?

~ Are the objectives attainable by these students?

~ Are the objectives in harmony with the philosophy of the school in which the instruction is to be given?

~ Are the objectives in harmony with basic principles of learning?[2]

A sixth question could be added to Gronlund's list:

~ Are the objectives in harmony with the teacher's perceived needs for the future of the child and of society?

Bloom's levels of understanding have helped in establishing objectives for almost half a century: Knowledge (remembering previously learned material); comprehension (grasping the meaning of material); application (using learned material in new situations); analysis (breaking material down into its component parts); synthesis (putting parts together to form a new whole); and evaluation (judging the value of material).[3] How these categories can be used directly by the teacher is illustrated by Gronlund **(Table 1, p. 29)**.

Preparing objectives is not always easy, even with help. But it is worthwhile because much of the teaching process then follows almost automatically.

The first time this writer sat down to prepare objectives for a seminar in learning disabilities, the size and difficulty of the task were immediately apparent. The only thing that was clear was that certain topics must be covered. But, what specifically should the students be able to do as a result of instruction in these topics? For example, one topic relating to learning disabilities is definitions. Previously, we had dealt in general goals such as "Students should be familiar with the major definitions of learning disabilities." This was about as specific and helpful in planning teaching activities as "children should have a variety of word attack skills." After much head scratching and help from the sources mentioned above, specific objectives began to emerge. Under the topic of definitions, the following objectives were developed, using Bloom's categories:

Definition of Learning Disabilities

1. Knowledge level: Write three major definitions and give the source of each.

2. Comprehension level: Using no technical terms, describe a child who would be classified by the Task Force I definition as having a learning disability.

3. Application level: Given case history data on three children, tell which definitions include and which exclude each child.

4. Analysis level: Cite three commonalities in all major definitions of learning disabilities and cite two factors on which there is wide disagreement.

5. Synthesis level: Write a new definition of learning disabilities which would be maximally inclusive.

6. Evaluation level: Given 10 definitions of learning disabilities, evaluate each in terms of its practicality for a school district.

This rather lengthy and personal illustration of writing specific objectives is offered to:

~ reassure the teacher that it can be done and is worth doing, and

~ show how Bloom's categories can be used to insure that objectives cover more than just rote recall and that teaching can include the "higher" cognitive processes such as application, evaluation, and synthesis. Too often we only stress the first levels of knowledge and comprehension.

Some teachers have been exposed only to behavioral objectives which deal with educational trivia and are understandably reluctant to operationalize their own classroom goals. It is actually much easier to write objectives at the knowledge level than at the higher levels of application through evaluation. But this is no excuse for failing to tackle the more difficult and more rewarding task of writing objectives which deal with important and far-reaching aims of education. In an eighth grade unit about the U.S. Constitution, students were required to match the numbers of the Amendments with a phrase describing each. Apparently, the objective selected by the teacher was "to memorize the number of each Constitutional Amendment." We can sympathize with the obvious difficulty of selecting a more important aim such as "describe how a recent event in your own life might have been different if the first ten amendments did not exist." But no one promised that good teaching was easy.

Specific objectives need not deal with trivia. They need not be limited to dealing with facts. They can be extended into the significant and complex areas of appreciation, enjoyment, and attitudes, as we will see later.

Table 1
Examples of General Instructional Objectives and Behavioral Terms for the Cognitive Domain of the Taxonomy (Gronlund)

	Illustrative General Instructional Objectives	Illustrative Behavioral Terms for Stating Specific Learning Outcomes
Knowledge Level	• Knows common terms • Knows specific facts • Knows methods and procedures • Knows basic concepts • Knows principles	• Defines, describes, identifies, labels, lists, matches, names, outlines, reproduces, selects, states.
Comprehension Level	• Understands facts and principles • Interprets verbal material • Interprets charts and graphs • Translates verbal material to mathematical formulas • Estimates future consequences implied in data • Justifies methods and procedures	• Converts, defends, distinguishes, estimates, explains, extends, generalizes, gives examples, infers, paraphrases, predicts, rewrites, summarizes.
Application Level	• Applies concepts and principles to new situations • Applies laws and theories to practical situations • Solves mathematical problems • Constructs charts and graphs • Demonstrates correct usage of a method or procedure	• Changes, computes, demonstrates, discovers, manipulates, modifies, operates, predicts, prepares, produces, relates, shows, solves, uses.
Analysis Level	• Recognizes unstated assumptions • Recognizes logical fallacies in reasoning • Distinguishes between facts and inferences • Evaluates the relevancy of data • Analyzes the organizational structure of a work (art, music, writing)	• Breaks down, diagrams, differentiates, discriminates, distinguishes, identifies, illustrates, infers, outlines, points out, relates, selects, separates, subdivides.
Synthesis Level	• Writes a well organized theme • Gives a well organized speech • Writes a creative short story (or poem, or music) • Proposes a plan for an experiment • Integrates learning from different areas into a plan for solving a problem • Formulates a new scheme for classifying objects (or events, or ideas)	• Categorizes, combines, compiles, composes, creates, devises, designs, explains, generates, modifies, organizes, plans, rearranges, reconstructs, relates, reorganizes, revises, rewrites, summarizes, tells, writes.
Evaluation Level	• Judges the logical consistency of written material • Judges the adequacy with which conclusions are supported by data • Judges the value of a work (art, music, writing) by use of internal criteria • Judges the value of a work (art, music, writing) by use of external standards of excellence	• Appraises, compares, concludes, contrasts, criticizes, describes, discriminates, explains, justifies, interprets, relates, summarizes, supports.

Writing Objectives

When we begin writing objectives, we usually have at least two important considerations in mind — the topic or general content area (written compositions, multiplication, phonics, weather maps) and how the student feels about the content and himself as a learner. We want the student to develop or maintain positive attitudes toward the subject matter. We might even be in the position of considering objectives which are themselves largely in the affective domain, e.g., changing Susan's low self-esteem.

The reading teacher not only wants to teach Mark to be a proficient reader but also hopes he will enjoy reading. We can now ask the magic question. What student behaviors will we accept as evidence that our general goal (understand weather maps, develop number concepts) has been reached? What will the learner be able to do that satisfies us he does indeed understand weather maps? Obviously, the specific objectives under the topic of weather maps would be different for a fifth grade introductory unit and for a college meteorology course. Just what do we want the fifth grader to be able to do about weather maps — recognize one, given a road map and a weather map? Draw one, given barometric readings? Predict the weather from one, with no greater inaccuracy than the local TV forecaster? Describe present weather by looking at the map? These all represent the beginnings of different, but totally legitimate objectives. And who must decide which ones are appropriate for a given student or class? It's the teacher, with as much student participation and negotiation as possible, who is finally responsible. Similarly, who must decide what constitutes evidence of a "good attitude" toward studying weather? Right again — the teacher, with the student's help. How could the teacher judge whether Harold has been "turned on" by studying weather? She would have to look at what Harold does. There is no other way. The teacher might note whether he volunteered in class discussion, turned his assignments in on time, brought a weather map to school, asked to build a wind vane in science class, checked out a library book on weather, or stayed in at recess to talk about clouds. The teacher might assess such behaviors for the whole class. If year after year the signs of positive interest in weather were few, the teaching activities obviously need revamping. The teacher might employ a new film on weather or sponsor a contest to see who is the best weather

Ozzie's Words of Wisdom

We want the student to develop or maintain positive attitudes toward the subject matter. We might even be in the position of considering objectives which are themselves largely in the affective domain, e.g., changing Susan's low self-esteem.

predictor, or bone up on weather so she has enough interest in the subject to pass it on enthusiastically to the children. It's difficult to be excited about something we know very little about. This, incidentally, illustrates one fallacy in teaching approaches which claim to center on children's interests. While we teach so that children can have a wide variety of interests, interest seldom exists prior to experience and knowledge.

To sum up what we have said so far:

~ We must develop specific objectives;

~ The process of selecting them requires careful thought and planning;

~ Preparation of objectives may be facilitated greatly by Bloom's work and other guides;

~ We usually begin with general topics or objectives and with the recognition that our objectives are not limited to content but also include developing attitudes.

Now we move on to even more specific guidelines for preparing educational objectives.[4]

Objectives Must be Behavioral

An educational objective must be so specific that a stranger to the classroom could readily determine if students had accomplished it. The objective must make it clear how to deal with what the student is able to do. While we are rightfully concerned with what he knows, believes, feels, understands, or appreciates, we must also look at what he DOES to understand the knowledge he possesses

> **Ozzie's Words of Wisdom**
> *An educational objective must be so specific that a stranger to the classroom could readily determine if students had accomplished it.*

and his "attitudes." We can only assess his knowledge, feelings or beliefs by looking at his performance. A music educator is interested in whether students learn to appreciate certain types of music. But the only way to make reasonable inferences about their appreciation is to examine their behavior — what they say or write about music, or the amount of time they spend listening to it. The primary teacher concerned with instilling a genuine liking for reading in her students looks at reading behaviors to judge whether they like to read. In other words, when we limit our objectives to behaviors the learner will display, we're not minimizing concern with the knowledge, feelings or beliefs that prompt the behavior; we are acknowledging that we must use behavior as the basis for our judgments. We have nothing else to use.

The first guide in establishing a useful objective, then, is that it must describe what the learner will DO when he has achieved it. Objectives, therefore, include verbs like list, name, identify, point, write, draw, construct, label, solve, match, and exclude such words as appreciate, understand, know, comprehend or realize.

Since most teachers have experienced a college-level course in reading instruction, we can use the course objectives as an example. If the instructor stated as an objective, "The students will know three different methods by which to teach beginning reading," observers might disagree on whether students had reached it. Did the instructor mean the students should name three methods (e.g., whole language, phonics, or eclectic), that they should be able to teach students to read by each of three methods, be able to write a four page description of the similarities and differences among three methods, or be able to match the names of three commercial reading programs with the type of method employed in each. It's only when the objective is stated in terms of what the learner will DO to "demonstrate competence" that we can evaluate how well it has been accomplished. The instructor benefits from having specific written behavioral objectives because he knows precisely what to teach and can evaluate the teaching. The students benefit because they know exactly what they're expected to learn. The student who knows she will be required to write a four-page summary of the earliest expeditions into the Oregon Territory can study more effectively than the one who is told, "you must fully cover the chapter on the Oregon Territory," and then is asked to match fur trappers with rivers and missionaries with mountains!

Ozzie's Words of Wisdom

It's only when the objective is stated in terms of what the learner will DO to "demonstrate competence" that we can evaluate how well it has been accomplished.

Givens or Conditions

Return to the example of the reading methods course. The instructor's intended objective was that the student "teach a group of children to read, using each of three different methods." Is that an adequate statement of the objective, describing a behavior the students will perform at the end of instruction? Would you and I agree on which students reached that objective? What if a student could teach a small group of seven-year-old faculty children to read with each of three methods, but couldn't teach a large group of disadvantaged five-year-olds to read? The objective, as stated, is inadequate because it doesn't delineate the conditions under which our student does the behavior. A better statement of the objective would be, "To teach three groups of eight typical six-year-olds to read, using three different methods."

Sometimes it's not essential to state the givens under which the behavior will occur; other times it's highly important. If the objective, for instance, were to underline 98% of the misspelled words on a theme written in class, it is hardly necessary to repeat "given a theme." It is apparent. If the objective were to teach children to bounce on a trampoline ten consecutive times without falling, the trampoline is in the objective without also being specified as a given. We must be prepared to carefully delineate the givens, but only when necessary.

Level of Performance or Criterion

What if four of our eight six-year-old children read at a 1.9 level following the reading instruction, two read at a 2.4 level, and two weren't able to score on the reading test we administered? Has our student teacher taught these children to read? We failed to specify in our objective the level of performance expected. We must add this element of the performance criterion if our objective is to be helpful. The objective, "To teach three groups of eight typical six-year-olds to read well enough that 75% of the students in each group score at or above grade level on the XYZ reading test, using each of three different methods," contains all three elements of Mager's instructional objectives:

~ identify and name the overall behavior act,

~ define the important conditions under which the behavior is to occur (givens or restrictions, or both), and

~ define the criterion of acceptable performance.[5]

There are times when it appears that an objective might be refined until it becomes ridiculously long and overly detailed. This is, in part, the nature of language. But if each teacher "writes" (not "plans," "intends," or "carefully thinks out") objectives in enough detail that an outside observer could easily determine if each child reached the objective, a vital job will have been done.

Objectives Determine Teaching Methods

Teaching method must be appropriate to the objective we have established. If, for instance, the objective were to have the children "determine by experimentation the effect of heat on four different substances of their own choosing," then the teacher would not lecture. The teacher would arrange the environment so children could choose, experiment and record efficiently. After students had accumulated data on the effects of heat on a variety of substances, the teacher shifts from the role of environment-arranger to that of generalization facilitator. If the original objective were to teach students to, "State the rule governing the relationship between the height of an air column and the pitch of the sound produced," then a direct, deductive approach might have been more efficient.

Efficiency in learning is highly important, and becoming more so every day as the knowledge explosion accelerates. We cannot afford to waste our children's precious time. We recall observing a fifth grade classroom in a reportedly excellent school where a 50 minute science period was devoted to filling bottles of various sizes and shapes with water and directing air streams into them. Chaos prevailed as the children shoved, spilled, couldn't see, and missed the critical moment when the air was finally blown into the bottles. All this was, according to the teacher, for the purpose of teaching the concept that the height of the air column was related to the pitch of the sound. Most

Ozzie's Words of Wisdom

The point is that the objective determines the style of the teacher's approach. Efficiency in learning is highly important, and is becoming more so every day as the knowledge explosion accelerates. We cannot afford to waste our students' precious time.

of us would agree that the concept could be taught much more quickly and with better retention in a number of ways. In all probability, most of the children already knew it! What ten year-old hasn't blown into an empty pop bottle to produce a fog horn sound?

The point is, the objective determines the style of the teacher's approach. The question is not one of structure versus lack of structure, or lecture versus discovery, or inductive versus deductive, or rote versus meaningful learning. It's choosing the style which produces the most efficient learning of the specified objective. This position is substantially different from the false claims that all approaches are of equal value and the only thing that matters is that the teacher is comfortable with the approach being used.

> *In our experience, many elementary teachers are reluctant to use direct, systematic, efficient teaching styles and rely excessively on student-directed, participatory learning. This may be due to the failure of teacher preparation programs to teach effective use of direct instruction methods while maintaining a high degree of student interest. At the secondary level, the opposite is often seen; teachers overuse direct teaching methods such as lecture and infrequently use participatory teaching styles.*

Let us close with one more example before each reader leaves us briefly to practice writing behavioral objectives. Indicate which of the following is a useful instructional objective:

In the following example, "the purpose of this chapter is to assist readers,"

1. . . . to become better teachers who enjoy their work fully and are developing to the maximum of their individual potentials, or

2. . . . to write their own instructional objectives, each containing the behavior the learner will perform, any essential conditions under which he or she will perform it, and the level of acceptable performance.

Task Analysis and Entering Behaviors

Chapter III

Once an educational objective has been established, we are ready to move to the next teaching step. The objective has been stated in the form of a task the children will learn to perform, i.e., they will write, draw, read, say, or construct something — a task which represents a new accomplishment.

This step asks, what are the sub-tasks, the steps or prerequisites to performing the new task which could not previously be done? Task analysis is the process of isolating, describing and sequencing all sub-tasks which, when the child has mastered them, will enable him to perform the objective. This is also known as designing instruction.[1]

The focus in analyzing the task is only on skills that are part of what we are trying to teach. The words minimal and essential could be used in place of necessary. Let us say, the objective was for the students to:

"Tell time to the nearest five minutes, given a non-digital clock."

The teacher might approach this task analysis by asking, "What are the teachable subskills which would insure that every child who had them could reach this objective?" Or she might ask, "What are the possible sources of error or confusion that could result in failure to achieve the objective?" A variety of ways can be used to approach the job of analyzing a task. Basically the approach is first logical and then empirical, which simply means that the teacher must figure it out the best way possible — drawing on reason, experts, curriculum guides, past experience with teaching related skills, knowledge of how children respond and perform in classrooms. Then, try it out with the children. It's just that simple, and just that difficult!

If we look back at our time-telling objective, one possible set of subskills that would guarantee the performance outlined in the objective would be as follows. Each child must be taught to:

~ Count by fives from zero to 60.

~ Discriminate the long and short hands of the clock.

~ Apply the rule that the short one "points" and the long one "counts."

~ Apply the rule that "the hands start here, go this way (clockwise), and if it isn't there yet, it isn't there."

~ Say the hour designated by the short hand, followed by the minutes (0 - 55) designated by the long hand.

Of course, there are other ways to slice the pie or divide the skills. The above way seems reasonably efficient. The crucial questions are whether all five subskills are necessary and whether they are sufficient to insure success in reaching the specified objective. Some teachers might protest that they would not have set such an objective in the first place, opting for a digital time-keeper instead. Fair enough. The point is, whatever the task, once it's determined, it should be analyzed or broken down, into its own necessary and sufficient subskills.

Many common classroom activities are closely related to valid objectives and it's easy to mistake them for essential ones. To illustrate, in a recent workshop, a group of primary teachers were given the following objective and asked to design an activity to teach it:

"Given the visual letter m, the child will respond with the sound /m/."

Several teachers suggested giving the student a worksheet depicting many objects and having him circle all those objects whose names begin with /m/. This activity might be appropriate for some other objective (try writing an objective for which it would be well-suited, just for practice), but it's only "related" to our objective above; it's not on-target. A child could do an infinite number of such worksheets without error and still be unable to fulfill the objective. Thus, the worksheet activity is neither necessary nor sufficient and isn't, therefore, a subskill to be listed under the objective.

When a teacher undertakes a task analysis, what does the finished product look like? For tasks such as arithmetic which often involves sequential learning, we might describe it as a "task ladder," with the top rung being the culminating step — our objective. Some objectives can be reached with little attention to the order in which the child masters steps, so that the analogy of a ladder, with the child moving sequentially from one step to another doesn't always fit. These task analyses have been called "pies," since when all the slices (sub-tasks) are in place, the pie is complete.[2]

Imagine for a moment that every teacher had in her possession a list of skills and concepts to be taught and it extended downward to include major prerequisite learnings, area by area. This can be readily visualized as a group of task ladders, probably arranged by content area. The primary teacher would have a task ladder for reading skills, for arithmetic, handwriting, classroom behaviors (including work habits, socially acceptable group behavior, etc.) and for social studies, science or health.

There can be several different ladders within a given area. In arithmetic, there could be one for facts, computational skills and story problem skills. The highest rung of a given task ladder is the specific instructional objective for that unit of instruction (the unit could be a year, a week, a lesson, or x number of pages in the workbook). Each prerequisite or related concept or skill occupies its appropriate rung.

Kameenui and Simmons present four writing strands (mechanics, writing simple sentences, writing paragraphs, editing) and the core skills within each. The core skills of writing simple sentences are:

~ Identifying a sentence as naming somebody or something and telling more about the person or thing.

~ Selecting sentences that name somebody or something and tell more about the person or thing depicted in the picture.

~ Completing sentences that name somebody or something and tell more about the person or thing depicted in a picture or series of pictures.

~ Generating sentences that tell the "main thing" that happened in a picture or series of pictures.

~ Generating sentences that name somebody or something and tell more about the person or thing without use of pictures.

~ Combining simple sentences to create more complex sentences.

These core skills would be taught sequentially. In their editing strand, Kameenui and Simmons include:

~ Identifying sentences that do not report on what a picture shows.

~ Correcting mistakes in capitalization and punctuation.

~ Identifying sentences in a paragraph that do not tell about a specified topic.

~ Correcting run-on sentences.

~ Correcting sentences with present-tense verbs by changing them to past-tense and writing all sentences in past-tense.

~ Correcting inappropriate noun-verb relationships and inappropriate pronouns.[3]

These skills probably need not be taught in any particular sequence. Several could be worked on simultaneously, rather than having to teach each to mastery, in order.

Examine the following task sequence and determine to what extent, if at all, the sub-objectives need to be taught in order:

Objective:

The child will add any two one-digit numbers without error.

Prerequisite (entering behaviors):

The child can hold a pencil, crayon, or chalk, make a straight vertical line and a plus sign.

Sub-objective 1:

The child counts from one to ten, including counting from a number other than one and counting to a number other than ten. For example, the child can count to 3, 5, 8, 10, and 2 and can count from 3 to 10, 2 to 5, 4 to 8, and 5 to 9.

Sub-objective 2:

The child counts one to ten vertical lines, where each line corresponds to one number and, conversely, the child can make the appropriate number of lines when told the number of lines to make, up to 10 and including zero lines.

Sub-objective 3:

The child uses the plus sign (+) to count consecutively two separate groupings of lines and responds to the plus sign by stating the total number of lines when the two groups are combined:

~ Reads a plus sign (+) correctly, i.e., child says "plus" when he or she sees "+."

~ Reads a number sentence with lines and a plus sign, e.g., reads /// + /// as "three plus three."

~ Reads a number sentence with lines and a plus sign, and then gives the correct answer. For example: //// + // is read as "four plus two equals," and the correct answer is then given.

One task analysis of beginning decoding, now unequivocally supported by extensive research is as follows:

Objective:

Given any regular CVC letter combination, the student will read it correctly.

Prerequisite:

Phonemic awareness, i.e., the ability to segment a spoken word into separate sounds and to blend separately presented sounds into a spoken word.

Sub-objective 1:

Given any letter, the student will say the appropriate sound.
(Note: this could be many separate objectives, corresponding to individual sounds or groups of sounds, such as vowels.)

Sub-objective 2:

Given a word or a line of print, the student will begin at the "left" and progress to the "right," whether those labels are used or not, saying the sounds (orally or silently) and then blending them into words.

The terms "objective," "prerequisite," "sub-objective," "skill," "task," or "goal" are all relative and arbitrary. What is a goal or objective in one task analysis can be a prerequisite for a more advanced task. Similarly, a prerequisite in one task could be a goal in the teaching of simpler tasks. One large "ladder" is a "scope and sequence" chart common to many texts. Unfortunately, curriculum materials differ tremendously from each other in the amount of knowledge about and attention given to the process of designing the instruction. The teacher who uses the well-designed materials known as direct instruction programs and receives adequate training in using them will be highly effective and will only rarely need to do additional task analyses. The effectiveness of "direct instruction" with regular and special education has been well established.[4, 5, 6, 7]

A thorough task analysis and ladder enables the teacher to determine quite precisely where to begin instruction geared toward the objective. Remedial reading teachers often observe that even middle school children referred for help in reading have less than perfect mastery of sound symbol relationships and even more frequently are unable to blend sounds together to form words. In all teaching, but especially so in remedial work, it's important to begin instruction at the appropriate level. This requires assessing the child's "entering behaviors." Task analysis provides an excellent and efficient means for doing this.

Assessment of Entering Behaviors

Global descriptions of the child's entering behaviors (for special education students these appear on the IEP and are called present levels of performance) include such common items as "He is ready for third grade," or "She has a developmental age of 8." While this provides some information for the teacher, it really isn't much more than what he can quickly size up for himself within the first few encounters with the child. A score of "45th percentile on the Wunmore Test of Somethingorother" similarly doesn't tell the teacher much she couldn't find out herself in more useful terminology. Even such "diagnostic" test data as "one year above grade level in reading, at grade level in spelling, and two years below grade level in arithmetic" doesn't really answer the twin questions of every teacher — "exactly **what** and **how** does the child need to learn?" All the kinds of data just mentioned derive from norm-referenced tests, with norms of one kind or another by which a child is compared to some group of children. These tests, at their best, may have a role to play in research or in placement decisions, but they are not very useful in teaching. It's time we face that fact squarely and stop assuming that something is wrong with the teacher who cannot translate standard scores, percentiles, or stanine scores into lesson plans. They just do not translate. Someday they may be translatable, but that day is not yet here. Clearly, therefore, we are not advocating that teachers look to these tests for relevant data on the entering behaviors of the children to be taught.

If we don't look to norm-referenced tests, where then do we look? Some texts, especially in child development and elementary education, would have us observe the child in a variety of situations, interview his family, take a social history, discuss him with the school nurse, read his medical records, read daily anecdotal records kept by his last four teachers, check his cumulative folder and discuss it with the school counselor, and so on. If it were possible to do this for 27 children prior to lesson #1 — which it is not — and if the data we would obtain were relevant — which they are not — then we might recommend this approach. But we do not. If we look to neither global norm-referenced tests nor to the shotgun, "find out-everything-from-every-body-about-every-child" schools of thought, what then?

If we had complete task ladders for each and every instructional objective and goal, the relevant entering behaviors for any given task would be all the rungs preceding the objective or the final task. To know what a child must learn before she can do subtraction problems of the kind we are teaching, we construct simple checklists with a test item for each rung on the subtraction ladder. The concept that the equal sign means we must count to the same number on both sides is relevant to the task of solving problems of the form

9 – 3 = X. Where a child's grandmother works and her IQ are not relevant. The rungs of the task ladder tell us what a child must be able to do to reach our objective, and that is what is relevant to the teacher. To put these pages in one simple-to-understand but difficult-to-implement rule: To assess relevant entering behavior, the teacher must determine prerequisites to a successful performance of the task the child lacks. This presupposes that the teacher knows the prerequisites of all major tasks. And that's the rub. It seems to this writer that some teachers, especially at the secondary level, most often err on the side of underestimating the importance of prerequisite skills. When a history teacher limits his presentation to telling the students to read Chapter II in class and be prepared for an oral test on the material, the ability of each student to read the assigned material is critical. And yet, it too often happens that not all students confronted with such assignments can read them.

Some primary teachers, on the other hand, tend to insert irrelevant tasks onto such basic ladders as reading. The act of reading (decoding) doesn't requires the student to be able to put an X on the geometric form different from the others, that she have a rich background of field trips, or be able to name the letters of the alphabet. And yet such activities are frequently labeled reading readiness or prerequisites to reading.

Meaningful Assessments of Entering Behaviors Require That the Teacher:

~ specify instructional objectives for the tasks to be taught,

~ list the essential subskills and/or prerequisites to each task,

~ construct a brief checklist of test items representing the subskills of each on the ladder, and

~ administer this checklist to the students.

This procedure, rather than relying exclusively on normative tests, interviews, or other diagnostic data will provide the teacher with a meaningful assessment of content-related entering behaviors.

Grouping

Task analysis can also be helpful in grouping students for instruction. Grouping should initially be done on the basis of specific tasks students need to be taught. In reading, those who haven't mastered the concepts of directionality (by this we mean only that we read and write in this direction ──────▶) and sequencing may be grouped for instruction in those concepts. Those who know directionality and sequencing but haven't learned the basic sound symbol relationships may be grouped together for that instruction. Ideally, children would be separately grouped for each educational task. In practice, those high on the rungs of one task ladder tend to be high on related task ladders, too.

After initial groupings are made, regroupings are done based on the rate at which students learn. The groups of faster learning children can be larger than slower moving groups. One of the problems teachers face in implementing flexibility in groupings is that students are aware of which groups move faster and which slower. In fact, when asked which reading group they are in, many reply "top" or "bottom" rather than describing themselves as a "bluebird" or "chipmunk." One way to reduce and possibly even eliminate this (at least in the lower grades) is by having partitioned or screened areas for small group instruction, to reduce the visibility of group activities. If this could be successfully done, the child moved to a slower group would have only good feelings about being in a situation where his success rate increased.

Describing student learning rates and things yet to be learned is preferable — factually, educationally, and humanistically — to older terms such as "bright," "smart," retarded."

Steps to Illustrate One Way of Forming Instructional Groups Based on Task Analysis:

1. The teacher makes a brief checklist of the 10-15 educational objectives considered most vital for her students to work toward during the first portion of the school year. These might include reading weather maps, solving long division problems or writing paragraphs with a main idea.

2. The teacher conducts a sample lesson pertinent to each item on the checklist, keeping the entire group together for the session.

3. On the basis of student responses to the lesson, those who have the most to learn before reaching an objective can be readily identified and formed into a group. A second sample lesson can assist the teacher in finding the next group. This procedure could be used to select as many groups as necessary, remembering that when it begins to be difficult to make discriminations among remaining students, they can be grouped together temporarily.

4. Often we must remind ourselves that some students will come to us with entering behaviors already higher on some task ladders than we had envisioned for most of the group after instruction. If a child can write a ninth-grade level composition in the fifth grade, it would be inappropriate to require him to punctuate sentences in a fifth-grade workbook. The sample lessons we propose for grouping purposes should also be used to find children for whom no additional instruction on a task ladder is appropriate. Such students can then be shifted to more advanced work, perhaps by individualized instruction or by being moved into a higher grade.

Task ladders can be helpful in teaching and to enable students to work independently. Each student can see the goal he is heading toward and grasp the role of subskills, some of which might otherwise seem fragmented or even useless. Students can move to more difficult tasks or rungs independently as they master each preceding level.

Peer teaching can be greatly facilitated by establishing guidelines for students assisting each other according to levels at which they are working. Teams and small groups can also be established this way. Individual progress records can be noted on miniature ladders. Teachers will be able to think of many additional ways task ladders can improve organization, achievement, and morale within the classroom.

A frequently raised question is whether homogenous or heterogeneous grouping is best. Common sense tells us that the more homogenous the group, the more efficiently instruction can be geared to the appropriate rung of the ladder. This is obvious. But the question isn't how children should be grouped for specific instructional purposes although that is how it is often worded. It's whether children should be placed in classrooms where students have a wide or narrow range of previous learning. The critical element is not the basis for placing students in the classroom, but what happens where they are placed. If a particular teacher had a good deal of interest, experience, and success using peer teaching (where students who had reached a certain rung of a task ladder were teaching students on lower rungs) she will function effectively with students who have a wide range of previous learning. On the other hand, a teacher who did a great deal with total-group, unison responses and class discussions, might do more with a homogeneous group. In sum, for direct instructional purposes, homogeneity is most efficient. For placement purposes, so many other factors enter in that homogeneity versus heterogeneity is not a major issue.

Readiness

In any discussion of entering behaviors, the term "readiness" is bound to arise. Our society is quick to coin new terms when they seem helpful or otherwise catch our fancy, making our dictionaries thicker each year. We are less quick to drop terms that have lost utility. "Readiness" may be a candidate for the lost-utility file, should we ever construct one. Everyone is ready to learn the next rung of any task ladder we might construct. If Robert is on rung 17 of the self-dressing ladder, he is ready for 18. If Mary is on rung 1, she is ready for 2. Since schools traditionally begin their relationship with children at ages 5 - 6 rather than birth, we haven't extended our ladders down into skills and concepts learned prior to school. So, in effect, school reading ladders begin at step 10 (or any other number) rather than at 1. When a child comes to us at age 6 and is on rung 4 instead of 10, we tend to say he "isn't ready for reading." What we mean is, we haven't thought about how to teach rungs 1 through 9 and aren't ready for him! He has further to climb than most 6-year-olds to reach the instructional objective, which is, "To say the appropriate spoken equivalent for visually presented groups of English letters. Therefore, he is the one who is most in need of teaching. And yet he is the one frequently told to wait a year until he is ready! If children can catch up with others ahead of them, we must teach them more, faster.

Let us either abandon the concept of readiness as we have used it in recent years — i.e., as a crutch or excuse for our failure to know how to teach sequentially and in small steps — or let us reformulate it as the description of tasks next in order to teach.

In the past, educators frequently took the position that the school is not ready to teach some kinds of behaviors and certain "immature" children would be excluded for a year. It was hard to demonstrate that a year at home taught those behaviors and students then possessed desired behaviors when they reapplied. Now, by law, programs must be available to developmentally delayed children at age three, and many birth-to-three programs are also available.

While all children are ready to learn, they aren't ready to learn it in a group setting, or sitting still, or when they must pay attention for many minutes. If a child has difficulty in a group setting, the best place to teach him the skills he lacks may be in a group situation. Again, this is the child who most needs to be in a structured program where the skills are taught systematically and sequentially.

Some of these issues have occurred in a sad but common scenario where the school personnel and the parents of a young child with autism differ about his placement. Parents often seek an in-home, intensive 1:1 training program where the child is taught such basic skills as imitation, making eye contact, and responding to other persons. The school often argues that the child needs to be in a school-based program where other children are present and socialization can occur. The parents respond that their child doesn't respond to others and doesn't imitate, so socialization won't occur until the prerequisite skills are learned. These are difficult questions.

Motivation

Each student can be described in terms of what she has already learned. This description includes pertinent skills and bits of knowledge which relate to a new learning area, attitudes and past experiences as a learner, expectations for failure or success in school tasks, feelings toward teachers and peers, and so on. Some part of this prior learning about tasks, about self, and about school is manifest as "attitude toward new learning." This is what we call "motivation." Older textbooks led us to think of motivation in terms of something within the child which he possessed in large or middling-amounts, or sometimes barely at all. An IEP which is currently being litigated provides that speech therapy for the frontal lisp of an IDEA-eligible student "will be discontinued until the student demonstrates appropriate motivation." In this IEP, all the responsibility for being sufficiently motivated is placed on the student, none on the therapist.

This view is hardly constructive since it fails to provide specific educational direction suggestions for the teacher. Some of the newer texts have taken a different direction, one which has more appeal, at least superficially. Here the emphasis is on the teacher motivating the children. The usual approach is to provide children with activities which they find interesting and are appropriate to their levels of development.

This Concept Has Three Drawbacks:

~ many student interests are learned, not innate;

~ the school curriculum is already designed to be appropriate to developmental levels, and

~ the teacher doesn't know if students will be motivated by a project until it's tried and their responses evaluated. But this leaves the teacher with an educationally un-useful concept. This only allows the teacher to say, after an activity, that the children were or were not motivated.

There is a more helpful way for the teacher to view the entire matter of motivation. A basic tenent of human behavior is, we do that which is rewarding and avoid that which isn't. Perhaps "satisfying" more accurately connotes the concept here than "rewarding." The Peace Corps worker who receives few tangible rewards for his efforts may find the job extremely satisfying. Most adults in our society have learned to value long-term satisfaction more highly than immediate, tangible rewards. Parents who sacrifice material acquisition for the sake of their child's education illustrate the principle of doing that which is satisfying. The child who chooses a gum ball over a dollar is operating by the same principle. The important thing for the teacher to understand is that children do those things which are satisfying to them. Some children are satisfied by the completion of a task itself, some by a grade, some by avoiding teacher's displeasure, some by a visual record of progress, or by free time earned through successful work.

The list of possible satisfactions following the completion of school work is almost endless. But what one child finds rewarding, another may avoid. The stories of gifted children feigning ignorance to avoid excessive teacher praise are not all myths. The teacher who thoroughly understands the role of reinforcement (satisfaction) in human activity can eliminate such dead-end statements as, "He is a poorly motivated student," and instead will ask, "What satisfying event or condition can I arrange to increase Elena's willingness to do this task?" Far from "bribery," as charged by some critics who do not clearly understand the principles of reinforcement, this an important, even critical, example of how principles of human learning can be used to enhance teaching. More will be said about these principles when we deal with behavior management.

Summary and Implications

Task analysis involves determining all subskills necessary and sufficient to lead to performance of instructional objectives. When the task analysis is complete, a checklist of test items corresponding to all subskills can be used to determine where to begin instruction, and children can be grouped according to the skills they need to learn. The task analysis approach to curriculum; diagnosing instructional needs, grouping children, and sequencing instruction, offers great promise to classroom teachers. An elementary school staff might begin by writing minimal educational objectives for all children moving from that school to the secondary level. These would constitute a summary statement of the school's intention to insure that by the end of elementary schooling, students could perform these skills or tasks at competency levels specified in performance criterion of objectives. Task ladders could then be devised containing all subskills which lead to accomplishment of objectives. Educational materials could be coded to show which subskills of which ladders they treated. Criterion-referenced test items could be developed to check which skills and concepts had already been learned and which needed to be taught. Grade level distinctions would be replaced by educational levels, rather than by physiological levels (such as chronological age). Teachers could specialize in developing materials and teaching strategies for particular task ladders or clusters of subskills. When children entered school, their proficiency levels would be checked out on major task ladders and they would be placed with other children learning the same new concepts and skills, under the direction of a teacher thoroughly knowledgeable in teaching those areas. Each child's individual program and progress record could be kept by showing daily or weekly, on his own set of task ladders, which tasks he had mastered and which remained to be taught. For some tasks, children could group themselves and work independently by referring to their task ladders.

A Framework Has Now Been Established for:

~ determining what is to be taught — educational objectives, and

~ delineating and organizing the steps of instruction.

The next area to be considered is the heart of the matter — how to teach. How do we arrange the environment so that Johnny and Mary move to higher rungs of each and every task ladder?

Teaching

Chapter IV

Primary teachers have been characterized as emphasizing children first and subject matter second, while the opposite is often said of secondary teachers. Teaching, as we see it, is always instructing somebody in something. The content is there and the learners are there. As the contrast suggests, the emphasis is sometimes more on the content or at other times on the student being taught. What we perhaps need is a guideline for when to emphasize how much of each. The more arbitrary the content, the greater the need to stress it and to develop a teaching methodology for all students; the more meaningful the content, the more emphasis can be placed on the unique experiences, needs and learning styles of each child.

Put another way, the greater the emphasis on the learning product (decoding words, solving algebra problems) the greater the need to focus on content and methodology; the greater the focus on the learning process (group problem-solving through discussion) the more the teacher can concentrate on each student being taught. The less diversity acceptable in the student's performance, the less appropriate in instructional methodology. The teacher who subscribes to such a distinction would instruct content such as beginning reading and arithmetic in a highly systematic and structured fashion while employing a variety of "looser" techniques and strategies in teaching social studies or art.

In today's rapidly changing world, there are still basic skills which facilitate the school and the after-school life of all children who master them. These skills should be taught in the most efficient and effective way possible. Reading, basic language usage, fundamental quantitative skills, and logic would be included in these areas of the curriculum. Of course, schools teach more than just basic skills; personal adjustment, social skills, creativity, values and more. Here the methods may be child-centered and vary greatly according to the child and the teacher.

Direct Instruction

The first section of this chapter deals with direct instruction only, and we recommend these procedures for those areas of the curriculum where objectives are clear and behavioral and the major focus is upon a specific performance of the student at the conclusion of teaching. Different approaches can be effective when the emphasis is on learner experiences during the process, e.g., a civics discussion where sharing ideas and listening to others may be more vital than the conclusions reached. We're not saying the entire school day should be spent in direct instruction, but when the goal is to teach all children certain basic skills in the most efficient way possible, these techniques are recommended.

With some modifications, the following sections on attention, task presentation, correction and reinforcement are based on the concepts of direct instruction developed by Becker, Engelmann, and Thomas.[1] These concepts have been validated by extensive and research and this approach is now recognized as an extremely effective teaching system.[2, 3, 4] The essential features of each act of direct teaching happen rapidly. Most complete task cycles, from gaining attention through reinforcement, require less than a minute. Many involve only a few seconds. In most direct instruction lessons each child responds between 0 and 10 times per minute. The steps below deal only with the direct teaching act itself. All necessary pre-planning, including setting of objectives, task analyses, room arrangement, grouping children, materials selection, scheduling and so on have already taken place.

Gaining Attention

Frequently we hear that the first step in teaching anything is to get the attention of those to be taught. But how seldom is this done? Why is this cardinal principle of good teaching violated so often? Because few of us teach exactly how to perform it. Getting the attention of all students isn't difficult, but it does require that the teacher act consistently. The ease with which children can be taught to pay attention depends on how much "opposite" learning they have already had. The instructor who begins teaching a group to pay attention in September will have an easier time than one who begins in April. Students too frequently learn that paying attention to what the teacher says isn't necessary and rewards can even be obtained by not doing it. Many students learn that if they don't pay attention when the teacher is presenting instructions or information, they will be rewarded either by individual teacher attention or by being allowed to get the information from another child. Children learn quickly that when they don't pay attention, they win more often than they lose. But how else can it be? How can the teacher be assured of having the attention of the students to whom she is about to teach something important?

Rules for Gaining Student Attention:

1. Always use a simple cue such as "listen," to show you are about to say something important. With young children use the same cue all of the time.

2. Never begin a lesson or an instruction until all students are attending.

3. Praise or otherwise reward these who attend immediately.

4. Never call attention to the child who fails to attend.

5. Insure that what you present to students is worthy of their attention.

Never and always seem like rigid recommendations. However, consistency in the use of the rules is essential. One violation on the teacher's part ("John, will you please stop shuffling your chair and pay attention," or "Harold isn't with us yet, is he, Class?") can undo weeks of patient and diligent work. Infrequent and unpredictable reinforcers can be amazingly powerful. The one time you slip and attend to the misbehaving child can ruin previous efforts.

The teacher who is about to begin direct instruction (on a important, interesting, and well-prepared lesson) might proceed like this:

~ "Listen." (Pause, because two children are not attending). "Look at how Mark is listening." He's really ready to work. Good listening, Mark. Listen." (She repeats the cue so that the children learn to respond to "listen," not to "good listening, Mark.")

~ Even though the first few days may require that the teacher spend more time obtaining the attention of all students than she would like to, the time gained in the long run outweighs the initial expenditure.

More than thirty years ago Becker, Engelmann, and Thomas[5] (1971) gave six still valid and useful steps for teaching young children to respond appropriately to the teacher's request for attention:

1. First, state the contingency — i.e., what will happen if the children perform. "Everybody watch me, and I'll show you a picture."

2. Pause.

3. Give the attention signal, e.g., "Watch me."

4. At the same time, use a hand signal to hold the children's attention. Hold the right hand out and look from side to side to check each child's attention. By moving the right hand one way while looking another way, it is possible to hold the attention of all the children better.

5. Next, give a social reinforcer for good attending. In praising the children, tell them what they are being praised for. "That's good watching."

6. Give any other reinforcer which was promised.

If even one child in the group fails to attend, it is essential to get his or her attention before proceeding with the lesson. This can be done by praising those children who are attending, by calling the attention of those who are not attending to the desired responses of the others. Suppose a child in the group truly did not know what "watch me" meant. It would be essential to show him what the expected behavior was and a very effective way to do this is by peer modeling. Be sure not to praise or give other attention which might be reinforcing to the child who was not attending.

Presentation of Content

Observations in some schools have shown relatively few minutes devoted to teacher presentation of new material. A larger amount of time is spent in behavior management and logistical concerns, such as distributing workbooks or lining up for recess. This part of our discussion is directed toward presenting new concepts, information or problem-solving strategies. The attention of the students is already focused on the teacher, the whiteboard, the screen, the book, or whatever the source of the information will be.

A primary consideration is how much clutter is acceptable in a presentation. From the viewpoint of direct instruction, the most common flaw in teacher presentations, from kindergarten through graduate school, is too much clutter.

Compare Two Presentations in Decoding:

T: *Now children, today we, are going to have a – guess what we're going to have – yes, we're going to have a new sound. Does anyone remember the sound we had yesterday?*

C: **It's / s-s-s/.**

T: *Yes, that's right but, class, did Jason raise his hand before answering? We always raise our hand, Jason. You try to remember that now. I wonder if anybody knows our new sound. It looks a little bit like a tree and that's how we remember it because it is the first sound in tree. We can hear it at the beginning of Tommy's name, too. Does anyone know what it might be?*

C: **Tee.**

T: *That's right. It's Tee and here's what it looks like. Jerry, please put your feet under your own chair and don't scrape them like that. We can't hear very well if you do that. Thank you. Now, here is our new sound (makes a t on chalkboard). Let's all say it together.*

C: *(Some shout /tee/, others say /t/ and some say nothing.)*

T: *Yes. This letter is tee and it says /t/. Now find your worksheet with ten trees at the top.*

Of course the above is an exaggeration, isn't it? Few of us are that cluttered. But on the other hand, do our presentations approach the clarity of the following example, based on DISTAR Reading I?

T: *All eyes are on the book. Good watching. This (pointing to t) is /t/. This is /t/. This is /t/ (pointing to another t). Everybody, what is this (pointing to t)?*

C: **/t/.**

T: */t/ That's right. Is this /t/? (pointing to a letter or symbol that is not t).*

C: **No.**

T: *Right. That's not /t/. Here's /t/ (pointing to t). What is this?*

C: **/t/.**

T: */t/. When I touch it you say it (rapidly pointing to several t's.).*

C: **/t/, /t/, /t/.**

The clutter in the first example occurred in dealing with minor behavioral matters which should have been ignored (feet shuffling) or averted (early, separate teaching of the rule about hand raising) and in off-task wordiness. The unfortunate results of cluttered presentations include: Failure to cover the desired amount of material, losing interest and attention and inadvertently misteaching or failing to teach. Student opportunities to respond are also greatly reduced. A crucial practice in presenting material is to prepare a clean, uncluttered presentation and keep it that way.

A presentation could conceivably be uncluttered but inaccurate or ambiguous, allowing some children to develop misconceptions. A primary consideration is whether the presentation is consistent with the real world about which we are trying to teach. This point is mentioned because of the rare teacher who violates it. Some bits of misinformation are relatively harmless in themselves, but can damage student confidence in the teacher who gives them. A second grade teacher who told the class that butterflies spread their wings after hatching from the cocoon to get the blood out of their stomachs was doubted by a gifted seven-year old and she remained skeptical all year. More serious is the case of the primary teacher who gives incorrect information about the sounds of letters when the child is attacking new words. Secondary teachers are often required to teach in an area outside their subject field. Any attempt to bluff or to stay one day ahead of the students is quickly found out and the class deteriorates to chaos or boredom. Better to admit that teacher and class will now be learning together, all as students.

A more frequent problem than giving misinformation is giving information which allows the child to form misconceptions. Most students already know a lot about common topics or tasks presented in school which reduces the number of misconceptions actually resulting from inadequate presentations. Unfortunately, this can cause us to blame the child who fails to grasp our presentation. For example, we are teaching the concept "red" to children recently arrived from Planet X where only shades of gray exist and no previous learning about color has taken place. The teacher holds up an apple, a red rubber ball, points to the flannel cut-out of a red circle, and draws a red chalk circle on the chalkboard, each time indicating, "This is red." She has a fair chance of teaching "red" to some of the students. The others could as easily conclude that "red" refers to roundness and call a tire "red." It is only the previous learning of our children that prevents this kind of disastrous result from occurring more frequently than it does.

Typical Results of Misteaching Include:

~ The students who consistently look at initial consonants and guess at the remainder of the word. ("Well, Debbie, what is the story about? What do you think that word might be?") They have learned what they were taught.

~ The students who divide fractions by their own rule of "turn something over and pretend it's multiplication," never having learned the underlying concepts.

~ The students who initially "reverse" symbols such as 7, 9, b, or d because they learned that how something faces (dogs, cars, people, etc.) makes no difference to what it is called.

The list is endless. These examples show why teachers must be sure their presentations are unambiguous and not dependent on previous learnings which have not been taught. To further emphasize this true essential of teaching, we'll present the concept of "chair" to the children of Planet X. The objective is to teach the concept of chair so that, "All of the children, presented with 50 objects, 10 of which are chairs, will answer with 100% accuracy the question, "Is this a chair?" If we teach that, "a chair is something to sit on," some children may misidentify the bicycle. What rule must we devise so that no child would incorrectly identify a sofa, stool, motorcycle, or toilet as a "chair?"

Some presentations rely so heavily on assumed prior learning that they are virtually useless for those who have not had the requisite earlier teaching. Most of us have had the experience of attending a convention session which was either so advanced or so unrelated to our interests we quickly left for the coffee shop or tried to find another session. The child in the classroom doesn't have that freedom. Nor does the teacher have the right, as convention speakers apparently do, to blithely proceed regardless of the gap between the presentation level and learner level. That's the difference, in a nutshell, between teaching and telling. The teacher who asks a child to list the major natural resources of Montana must be prepared to teach "list," "major," "natural," "resources" and "Montana." Just using the words or talking about them is not necessarily teaching.

In sum, the clean teaching presentation is uncluttered, accurate, unambiguous, and does not rely unduly on previously learned material. Someone once said better teaching would result if we assumed the learner was devoid of memory.

Correction and Reinforcement of Student's Responses

One of the best known and most frequently ignored principles of good teaching is the need for immediate feedback on the correctness of the student's response. If a person were given a task such as estimating the weights of the first 50 people to cross an intersection or to draw fifty lines each seven inches long, performance would not improve from the first to the last effort without information provided about the accuracy of his efforts. Some of the greatest abuses of the principle of immediate feedback occur in college courses where there often is no feedback at all until the final examination (which may not even be returned to the student). There the only feedback is the letter grade received after the term is completed. Yet, even the common elementary school practice of correcting and returning work by Friday is still a step away from the immediate revealing of results.

Careful use of group oral responses is one of the most effective ways to insure immediate correction or reinforcement. The group (usually three to ten children) responds together on cue from the teacher. After the group seems firm on the correct response, individual students can be queried. This gives all students a chance to practice or rehearse the correct response with the support of the group before being "tested" by individual performance.

Your goal is to maximize the likelihood that each student can respond correctly and to provide immediate (within seconds) information about the acceptability of her response. It's also important that when querying individual students, the question is asked before the child's name is said. If you say, "Mateo, what sound is this (pointing)?," the other children tune out as soon as the name is said.

A prevalent misconception about correcting a student is that psychological harm is done when he is told plainly that his response is erroneous. The fact is that calm, objective correction has not been shown to be harmful. Sarcasm, ridicule or other unduly punitive correction is potentially devastating to a student, and must be avoided. But to respond to a wrong response with a simple "No," followed immediately by the correct response or a clean prompt leading the student to the right answer is highly effective and in no way harmful.

When an errant response (group or individual) is given, the direct instruction teacher immediately corrects it, or reinforces it if it's right. Some teachers have a tendency to be too lenient in accepting partially correct responses. The motive in such cases is admirable — to leave the child with a positive feeling and some measure of success. But, this often derives from an exaggerated fear the child will be hurt by correction. If the teacher says "Johnny, that was a good try; it's kind of like a multiplication sign. We'll come back to it tomorrow," Johnny has been reinforced for a less-than-right response and next time will tend to repeat exactly the same response. Better to say "No, Johnny, this is a 'plus' sign. Right now this is hard to remember, but soon you'll always know it's a 'plus' and it will be easy for you. Plus, plus, plus. Got it? We'll come back to it tomorrow and you'll remember it's plus." When correcting a student, always emphasize the right response. Seldom is it wise to repeat a wrong response when correcting it.

Another common error in correcting a child is the failure to give the right response. Instead, too often when a child makes an error on material we believe the child "should" know, we say "John, look at that problem again," or "Now think about it more carefully" or "You know better than that. What does that really say?"

Effective Correction Procedures Include:

1. Give the correct response immediately. This is appropriate for "careless" errors, and errors of factual recall.

Examples:

T: *What sound is this (pointing to m)?*

C: **/n-n-n/**

T: *No – it's /m-m-m-m/*

T: *What is this numeral (pointing to 0)?*

C: **Nothing.**

T: *Zero. Zero. We call this numeral Zero.*

T: *What is the capital of New York?*

C: **New York City.**

T: *No, Albany is the capital of New York.*

A great reluctance to simply give children the correct answer can be observed in many teachers. It's as if we've been taught that giving answers is certainly not teaching and possibly is even akin to cheating. Part of the confusion may stem from failure to detect when an answer can more appropriately be reasoned from when such efforts are futile or too slow.

2. Give prompts or cues which lead the child to the correct response. The critical factor is the decision that the cues offered will be effective. The use of cues assumes the child has learned the material on which they are based. A successful use of prompting is seen in this example:

T: *Jimmy, solve this problem (3 + _ = 7).*

C : 10.

T: *What is this (pointing to equal sign)?*

C: Equal sign.

(NOTE: At this point, the teacher must be sure Jimmy has been taught the equal sign and the rule asked for next.)

T: *What does the equal sign tell us?*

C: "As many as we count to on one side we have on the other side." Oh, I see, it should be 4.

T: *Four, that's right. 3 + 4 = 7. You used the equal rule and it really helped you.*

3. Go through the correct response with the child. This is appropriate when the child is not yet capable of answering correctly by herself.

T: *Susan, count to 5.*

C: One, two, three, five.

T: *Listen to me count to 5. One, two, three, four, five. Do it with me.*

T & C: *(Counting together, with teacher leading strongly, emphasizing three, four, five.)*

When a child gives the right response, whether before or after correction, the teacher must reinforce it. More will be said about reinforcement in the section on Behavior Management. Our immediate concern is with techniques which will increase the chances the student will make the correct response again, will find that the response was worth the effort required to make it, will believe that he is capable of succeeding in school, and will know that learning can be fun.

Guidelines to Insure These Outcomes Include:

1. Reinforce immediately.

2. Use praise liberally, but not exclusively. A video tape was viewed in which the teacher mumbled "very good" after every correct response. The inflection and low pitch were identical every time. The children were no more reinforced than if the teacher had been clearing her throat. Some evidence suggests praise need not be sincere to be effective. However, we believe sincere, enthusiastic approval to be preferable.

3. Specific praise is more effective than general praise. "Good remembering the equal rule," "Class, listen to John count to 40 by 5's. He really knows how to do it," "Mary, I'm really happy you kept your hands on your own desk all period. That will help you work better," are more specific than "Good for you, Harry."

4. Use a variety of reinforcers. As children become more and more proficient and successful in school tasks, simply moving to the next task is reinforcing. Light hearted joking and creative teacher approaches can be highly effective. If children are learning slowly and with great effort, tangible reinforcers may be temporarily effective. Repeating the correct response is also a reinforcer, and should be done as a matter of course, regardless of whether other reinforcers are used.

5. A reinforcer is only a reinforcer when it actually works. Praise or raisins or gold stars or new tasks or anything else may have opposite effects on the behavior of two different children, and the teacher must constantly check that intended reinforcers are actually effective. This point has become clear to direct instruction teachers working with cultural groups in which performing well in front of the group is seen as show-off behavior and humiliates children in front of their peers.

6. The general rule is that learning new responses is work. Effort is required of the learner and if that effort isn't worthwhile to the learner, it won't be repeated. Reinforcement is essential to most learning and the teacher is one source of it. It's the teacher's responsibility to insure that correct responses are reinforced, one way or another.

7. Positive consequences are preferable to unpleasant ones. It's much better to reward correct responses than to punish incorrectness. Promising that negative consequences will result unless the children work hard is almost never necessary, though commonly used. Many consequences are implied rather than direct. A classic negative example is, "If you don't finish your arithmetic, you know what will happen." More effective is, "When we have

all finished, we're going to have a brand new game. Who would like some help in finishing quickly and accurately?"

Behavior Management

Behavior management is to classroom behaviors as direct instruction is to basic skills, and it has several principles which must be mastered by the teacher. In a well-managed classroom, students and teacher alike enjoy schooling far more than in its opposite. Equally important is that more time is available for teaching the curriculum when your energy isn't required to deal with nonproductive behaviors. Effective behavior management skills are a major support for teaching skills.

One goal for most teachers is to have a classroom atmosphere conducive to ongoing learning activities. At times this might mean substantial movement and talking; at others restrained and quiet movement. How is it that some teachers have classrooms where students seem to know what is expected? Some classrooms are in perpetual chaos and turmoil while in others disruptions are rare, minor and brief. Some teachers have all the luck — or is there an element of skill in behavior management? In fact, there are behavior management techniques which consistently enable teachers to have pleasant and productive classrooms.[6]

One general principle that works wonders is emphasizing "desired" behaviors. Few teachers deliberately create a negative atmosphere in their classrooms and yet one often develops. An observer in the typical class, tallying teacher praise for desired behaviors ("Jim, you did a beautiful job of sticking to your work when Mrs. Upset's class passed by our door") vs. attention given to undesired behavior ("Leonard, we don't hit people, do we?") finds more negative than positive comments. The first rule for teachers who want more efficient behavior management is to "catch" the youngsters being good. The teacher who tallies her own rate of "praises" and "blames" and makes the effort to use at least ten praises for every blame will be more than rewarded. Learning to use more praise requires recognizing the need to do so, since most of us are unaware how frequently we draw attention to undesirable behavior. But, be aware that when we begin to use praise in new circumstances, it may sound stilted or awkward. As we said earlier, research on this problem is reassuring. Even praise which sounds affected to adult observers, and is given less than enthusiastically may still be highly effective.

A second principle is to have few, but clear, rules for acceptable classroom behavior which are well known to all. Often students can successfully develop their own rules for the kinds of behavior they want in their room. Once codified, they should be stated positively and posted, and learned by each child. If possible, rules should number no more than five.

Rules Classroom Teachers Report to Be Successful:

1. Listen well.

2. Raise your hand before talking.

3. Be a good neighbor.

4. Walk in the classroom.

5. Sit quietly when you work.

During planned group activities and various other times the class may temporarily modify or suspend its rules, but they are always there as needed. In addition, they must be stated in age-appropriate language.

When a student repeats a given behavior over a period of time, rule of thumb is that something is reinforcing and maintaining it. We just do not persist in behavior that has no worthwhile or pleasant consequences. The gambler would not continue gambling unless he won at least once in a while. Yet, often the most effective reinforcer is one received only occasionally. The parents who accidentally taught their young child to cry, demand numerous drinks, call to them, and so on after being put to bed at night, did so by eventually giving in to the demands for attention. The child learned that if he cried loud enough and long enough someone would respond. Eventually, they came to understand that just as they had accidentally taught these behaviors, they could unteach them. They began the long, frustrating process refusing to reward the behaviors, no matter how long or loud the cries. The parents survived the ten day ordeal and the behavior had not occurred for a month. Uncle Charlie babysat one evening and the youngster reverted to his old ways. Unfortunately, Uncle Charlie produced the drink of water and two extra bedtime stories. The behavior was reinforced by this slip and now took 15 nights to re-extinguish it. Consistency is the essence of behavior management.

Whenever we ask a student to learn a new skill, solve a problem, or find a more mature way of dealing with interpersonal relations, we are asking him to exert energy. For the energy to be willingly given, there must be an adequate payoff. In ideal circumstances we can urge that every task should be rewarding in and of itself. But, some tasks which may eventually be rewarding (such as reading) are not immediately so for the child. There are lessons that possess neither immediate nor long-term utility. (When did you last use your diligently acquired skill of naming the capital cities of all the states, expanding a binomial, or calculating the height of a tree from the angle of the sun and the length of the shadow?)

Some teachers are most rewarded by working with children who already find it worthwhile to perform school tasks eagerly, regardless of the inherent interest or utility of the tasks. But many children find that some tasks aren't worth the cost in energy or time. In such cases the teacher must first determine that the performance being requested is worthwhile, even though the child may not be in a position to judge this. Once the task is established as necessary and worthwhile, decide whether exercising sheer adult power is appropriate. When it's not, the question then is how to make the task worthwhile for the youngster. One answer is carefully selected reinforcers. Historically, the consequences used in school were grades and punishments. For a variety of reasons these have not always achieved the desired results. Teachers are now using a greater variety of consequences with much better results. In classrooms all over the country students are busily working for diverse rewards: Free time, tokens, personal best performance records, points, opportunities to tutor other children, to listen to music, to invite classroom visitors, or to go on field trips. And, yes, cleaning erasers and passing out workbooks still appeal to some children.

One approach to insuring the value of tasks to students is the token economy. In addition to being successful, token economies are relatively easy to administer. Intuitively, good teachers have been using them for years, but under a different name. Here, students earn points, checks, coupons, or values toward activities or merchandise. One teacher found the merchandise earned in the class store to be so motivating to the students, they were using real money to buy the play money accepted at the store! This was quickly remedied by initialing the play money as it was earned by each child. Token economies can be highly individualized so that each child earns according to her own improvement. For example, in a class plagued by idiosyncratic spelling, a system was instituted in which some students received points for decreasing spelling errors, while others earned points only for errorless work. Spelling teams, comprised of good and poor spellers also worked together to earn team points.

Teachers who have not yet systematically used principles of reinforcement may feel it shouldn't be necessary to arrange consequences which result in better work. Children ought to be diligent, polite and successful in school because it's the way to be. We are reminded of the mythical business owner who purportedly believes that employees, "ought to be reliable, thorough, efficient, honest and loyal" regardless of below minimum wages, and no fringe benefits. Or the irate citizen who at school budget election time is heard to argue that teachers, "ought to be dedicated and devoted to teaching regardless of crowded classrooms, low salaries, and second-class citizenship."

When the job needs doing, the competent supervisor, boss, or teacher will insure the conditions which will get the job done efficiently, pleasantly, and well.

Some hold that the systematic use of behavioral principles to enhance productivity in the classroom is authoritarian and undesirable. While the professional teacher is indeed responsible for the outcomes of instruction, this does not imply or require a dictatorial approach. Students can be taught to set appropriate conduct and achievement standards for themselves and to select increasingly lower reinforcement levels. A second grader whose teacher was maintaining a well-planned token economy told her one day, "These subtraction problems are getting pretty easy for me now. I think I better do two pages, instead of one, to earn my chip." He was close to the day that his satisfaction in successfully doing arithmetic would be sufficient reward and the chip would be forgotten.

Many volumes have been written about behavioral principles, but one needn't study them all in order to use some effectively in the classroom. The essential underlying concept is that most human behavior is affected by its consequences. How-it-all-turns-out plays a large part in how-likely-we-are-to-do-it-again. In order to use this principle — consequences affect behavior — effectively in the classroom, we must often apply it in reverse. That is, we must recognize that a behavior occurring repeatedly tells us its consequences are maintaining it. Often the consequences that maintain desired classroom behavior are operating at home via parental approval for acceptable school performance or the reverse. And just as often, consequences which maintain undesirable behavior are operating right there in the classroom. Teachers may find it difficult to believe that their disapproval, however it is expressed, is actually causing children to continue misbehaving. Yet, this is exactly what frequently happens. One fifth grade ringleader candidly admitted that, "We just do that stuff so we can watch old man Richardson get mad." The moral is, we never know what is reinforcing for whom until we examine relationship between the behavior and consequences. What is positive to one child — e.g., the teacher's verbal praise calling class attention to the student's work — may be aversive to another. The same is true for adults.

Suppose the school principal determined to improve the accuracy and promptness of lunch money reports prepared by each teacher and offered the opportunity to work for two weeks in July on a paid public relations committee as incentive for preparing the reports. This offer would have a different effect on an independently wealthy teacher who spends July in Tahiti, vs the teacher who desperately needs the extra income.

A seventh grader with no previous history of school misbehavior was falsely thought to have been involved in a serious incident and was exiled for a week to the eighth grade room of the teaching principal who was known as a stern task-master. The remainder of the year the student misbehaved in an effort to once again be "punished" by exile to the more challenging and interesting eighth grade room.

In determining the effect consequences have on given behaviors, it's essential to keep records. Sometimes our perceptions fool us. A teacher referred an elementary child to the school counselor because he continually disrupted the classroom. The counselor asked the teacher to keep a record of the number of times these behaviors occurred, and to keep a baseline on a child who wasn't disruptive. Much to the teacher's surprise, she found the two children to be equally disruptive. The real problem was the referred child's failure to work independently and to complete assignments. The teacher's resulting frustration clouded her perception of other behaviors.

Another important reason for keeping records is that the process alone can have a positive effect on the behavior or performance in question, especially when children can meaningfully keep their own records and set realistic goals.

Principles of Behavior Management That Help Classroom Teachers:

~ Make absolutely sure students know what is expected of them by:

~ praising, drawing attention to, and otherwise rewarding desirable behaviors of all kinds and minimizing any attention to undesirable behavior, and

~ teaching a few clear, comprehensive, positively stated rules for classroom behavior.

~ Utilize the fact that when a behavior persists, the consequences of that behavior can be inferred to be positive to the learner.

~ If we want a behavior to occur again, the performance of that behavior must be worthwhile. Not all tasks are initially worthwhile in and of themselves. Something else, be it raisins or records of progress, must be used in the interim.

Managing Classroom Time and Space

Other overlooked aspects of classroom management are physical space and time management. A candle making workshop which employed young adults with mental retardation was visited by a management consultant team. After a few hours of observation they were able to make specific recommendations regarding the physical arrangement of the equipment, scheduling of breaks, handling of the token economy for worker rewards, the ordering processes, and materials storage which resulted in immediate improvements in production and morale. How many teachers could also benefit from expert assistance in arranging and managing the classroom? Sometimes an act as insignificant as moving the pencil sharpener eliminates disruption.

Some aspects of classroom management that might yield the greatest improvement in morale, atmosphere, or work accomplishment go unnoticed. Studies in the classroom have often shown that only a small portion of each day involves actual teaching. Could teaching time be increased? In all probability it can, but it's difficult for the teacher to see ways to do this.

A first step might be to obtain records of how classroom time is spent. An observer could keep detailed records more easily than the teacher, but even without this help it would be worth your time to do it. Make a time chart with space to record each minute. Devise a code; e.g., TG for teaching group, TI for individual teaching, M for directing pupil movement to recess, B for bookkeeping chores such as attendance and lunch money, P for preparation including organizing and finding materials, D for disruptions such as fire drill, announcements over the loud speaker, and so on. For many teachers it would be essential to include a category for dealing with non-academic pupil behaviors. Minute by minute records are necessary because so much of the time we spend inefficiently occurs in frequent, brief distractions. One approach could be, on Monday record the first hour of the school day, on Tuesday the second hour and so on. If the school could arrange video taping of two or three complete teaching days, the time analysis could then be made accurately and easily. Perhaps a group of teachers interested in finding ways to increase the proportion of their day spent in teaching could band together and request that in lieu of the next planned workshop, the district provide for observations and recommendations by consultants.

Even on a do-it-ourselves basis, a little time spent taking a hard look at present practices, known trouble spots, and possible solutions might prove rewarding. For instance, if we sketched the floor plan of our room, indicating desks, tables, library area, reading group, materials storage, and showed "traffic patterns" by time of day, we might get some ideas about rearrangements that could reduce confusion, congestion and time spent in transition from one activity to another.

One suggestion from instructors who use peer teaching is to set up several pupil directed "teaching stations" in the room where students go for individual help, for needed materials and further directions. This greatly reduces demands on teacher time. While we propose no panacea for the logistical problems of a busy classroom, the teacher who senses a need for greater efficiency could profitably gather data on the present situation (record of how time is spent, sketch of room arrangement, traffic flow) and compare it to the desired situation. Simple as these steps sound, we often stop short of them and allow ourselves to be pacified by an occasional grumble. Yet, it's relatively easy to bring about improvement by just going one step further. Anything that makes the complex job of teaching easier, simpler, more fun and more successful is surely worth considering.

Fluency – An Essential Goal

When direct instruction and effective classroom management have been properly combined, students have the best possible opportunity to reach proficiency in the skills they are taught. It's only when we are proficient, automatic or "fluent" in a skill that we can move to the higher levels of application and enjoyment. This makes fluency one of the most desirable outcome of our teaching-managing efforts.

Fluency refers to an easy fluidity of task performance. For example, one who reads orally at the same rate she speaks is a fluent oral reader and can put her cognitive energy into reading with expression appropriate to the meaning. In reading, fluent decoding is performed with automaticity, i.e., the decoding is done automatically, allowing the reader to focus on comprehending and enjoying the material. Fluency in handwriting, keyboarding or spelling allows the writer to focus on the ideas rather than the mechanics of getting words on paper. It's no stretch to say that Michael Jordan's movements on the basketball court or Itzak Perlman's violin playing are "fluent."

In contrast, think about the performance of the student first learning to drive, play a violin, speak a second language or read. Those performances are labored, uneven and error prone.

Until a learner reaches fluency in a given skill, that skill cannot be fully useful. One of the most striking individual differences in learning is the rate of reaching fluency in a new skill. Unfortunately, those learners who need more time to become fluent often do not receive it and instead are presented with yet another new task. The value of practice and more practice is universally accepted in musical and athletic endeavors. Practice in education skills, while just as important, has not always received such approval. "Drill and kill" expresses the disdain some educators have mistakenly had for practice to the level of mastery or fluency. In the past, standards of accuracy, e.g., 75% correct, have received far more attention than has fluency.

One reason for the rapidly growing acceptance of the role of fluency is that teachers now have easy access to fluency standards.[7] One source has always been there, but was seldom accessed until the work of Lindsley,[8] Haughton,[9] Starlin,[10] Binder,[11] and others focused attention on the fundamental importance of fluency. The readily available source we referred to is your own class of students. In one minute, a teacher can learn each student's rate of copying letters or numbers, solving arithmetic facts, writing words, etc. The students who need more practice to reach the class "norm" are easily identified.

Similarly, those who have studied fluency extensively have provided target rates. The chart in **Fig. 1** presents a sampling of rates from a variety of sources. It is not unusual to find slightly differing targets suggested or found in different studies. Hasselbring[12] observed that:

Fig. 1
Approximate Rates for Fluent Performances

Adult Fluency Rates:

Oral reading	200 - 300 words per minute
Writing letters	100 - 150 letters per minute
Math facts (e.g., multiplication)	80 - 110 facts per minute

Letter Sounds presented in random order: *(response, given letter symbols)*

20 per minute/0-5 errors	minimum
50 per minute/0 errors	fluent
30 per minute	before moving to new material

Spelling from Dictation:

4th grade	45 letters sequenced correctly per minute

Writing from Story Starter:

4th grade	16 words per minute

Oral Reading *(always with at least 95% of all words correct)***:**

1st grade target	60 words per minute
2nd grade target	110 words per minute
3rd grade target	145 words per minute
Adult target	200 - 300 words per minute

Math Skills:

1st - 4th grade reading numbers	80 digits per minute
5th grade + reading numbers	120 digits per minute
Student writing numbers	50+ digits per minute
Adult writing numbers	100 - 150 digits per minute
Student number facts (+,-,x,â)	60 - 80 facts per minute, saying or writing
Adult number facts (+,-,x,â)	80 - 100 facts per minute, saying or writing

"Most cognitive scientists now believe that as basic skills are practiced more, their execution requires less cognitive processing capacity, or attention, and becomes automatic. This is the concept of automaticity (fluency). All people have a limited capacity for information processing, If they do not have to use part it for performing basic skills, there is more capacity left to execute higher level skills. Thus, it appears that the ability to succeed in higher level skills is directly related to the efficiency with which lower level processes are executed."

Learners who become fluent are then better able to retain, to maintain performance over time, to transfer learning and to attend to tasks. They also are far more likely than non-fluent performers to enjoy the activity and learn independently. Surely these reasons to promote fluency are persuasive. Strategies for increasing fluency include: Emphasizing rate; providing positive consequences for increases in rate; increasing practice and drill; increasing number of response opportunities; changing the aim or goal rate; and providing consequences for incorrect responses. Oral reading fluency is enhanced by repeated and monitored oral passage reading and has not been shown to be improved by silent, independent reading.[13]

Supporting the Teacher

Just as it takes a village to raise a child, so even the most skilled teacher needs and deserves many supports to maximize the outcomes of education. Among these are top-notch administrators and special services personnel, appropriate budgets, safe buildings, cooperative parents and more. Among the important supports with which the teacher has the most contact are educational materials and personnel such as

Teachers See Themselves as Scapegoats

WASHINGTON – Committed but dispirited, most teachers say they are unfairly blamed for school shortcomings, undermined by parents and distrustful of their bosses, according to a study by Public agenda, a nonpartisan policy research group that has tracked teacher opinions.

More than three in four teachers surveyed said they were "scapegoats for all the problems facing education."

Wary of political favoritism and unfair claims by parents, teachers bank heavily on union support and on tenure policies that promise job security, the survey say. Such reliance comes even as teachers acknowledge flaws in the system: Only 14% said it was easy for their district to remove bad teachers, and 78% said their schools had at least a few.

Teachers also show some willingness to embrace change, such as paying higher salaries to those who put in more effort. New teachers, in particular, show support for options such as charter schools and alternative teacher certifications.

Eugene Register Guard

paraprofessionals, volunteers, and private tutors who also perform teaching or quasi-teaching functions.

Educational Materials

Ideally, every teacher has ready access to sufficient educational materials and evaluations of them, can select or modify and construct materials appropriate to specific objectives and can evaluate the effectiveness of materials. In practice it's often true that the teacher has great difficulty in obtaining new materials, finds it impossible to obtain any evaluative information beyond the publisher's advertising, has little time to construct new materials, and seldom evaluates materials in terms of meeting behavioral objectives.

Educational Publishing

Educational materials available in the commercial market place have proliferated in recent years. Obtaining and examining copies of new texts, kits, tests, boxes, workbooks, gadgets, and gimmicks could well be a full-time job. A small portion of these new materials have been adequately field-tested and evaluated prior to publication. The eventual question a profit-making business must ask about a product is whether it will sell. Publishers vary in the extent to which they ask other questions such as what evidence says this material successfully solves an educational problem.

Often when representatives of publishing companies visit schools they meet with staff other than the classroom teachers. They may leave examination copies of selected materials in the teachers' workroom, but this system is far from perfect. Many publisher catalogs are online as well as available by request, and teachers should take advantage of this. One of the most frequently cited benefits of conventions is the exhibit area where teachers may examine the newest materials and sign-up to receive mailings from publishing companies. School administrations should urge teachers to attend meetings featuring exhibits and facilitate their so-doing.

> ## Ozzie's Words of Wisdom
> *One of the most frequently cited benefits of conventions is the exhibit area where teachers may examine the newest materials and sign-up to receive mailings from publishing companies. School administrations should urge teachers to attend meetings featuring exhibits and facilitate their so-doing.*

In addition to getting on mailing lists, attending convention exhibits and seeking contact with publishers' representatives, teachers can subscribe to carefully chosen professional magazines, some of which do an outstanding job of presenting information about new materials.

A word of caution is due, however, about assuming that "new" is better, or even that it is good. By definition, new materials haven't been around long enough to have the track record, formal and informal, that older materials have. Also, we must be on guard against believing there is always a better mousetrap just brought to market or about to be. It's probable that we have already learned how to teach some basic things that haven't changed significantly for centuries, such as multiplication tables, sound-symbol associations or manuscript printing. We don't need to reinvent every wheel every year.

Evaluation of Published Materials

The new focus on accountability has revealed a lack of careful evaluation of many materials until long after they have been on the market and sometimes not even then. The previously uncritical acceptance of many materials is rapidly diminishing. Some years ago a popular program to develop visual perception seemed to many to offer the promise of improving early reading. After the program had been used with hundreds of thousands of children, it was found that progress in the product wasn't related to reading achievement although the children did improve in visual perception. Similarly, some rather expensive language development programs have been found to produce only a few or temporary gains in language usage skills. Some education officials are beginning to demand that data on program effectiveness be published with, not after, the materials. In fairness to those educational publishers who have diligently tried to provide teachers and children with practical and useful materials, it should be emphasized that educators have not only been willing to purchase and adopt materials without data, but have ignored data when they have been provided. Jeanne Chall reported in her famous *Learning to Read: The Great Debate* that not once in her extended experience did she encounter an instance where results of research influenced educators' decisions about selecting a reading program![14] Many research-oriented educators support her observation with their own experience in the futility of employing data to persuade practitioners. But this era of ignoring or down-playing data is hopefully part of the past. Both IDEA and NCLB appear to require that we employ scientifically validated educational materials, methodologies and programs.

However, most courts in the past have not interpreted IDEA in this way, although there is some reason to hope this trend may be changing. It remains to be seen whether the NCLB requirement will be enforced. The Reading First program is the academic heart and soul of NCLB. Under NCLB, states must insure that reading first funding goes only to schools that use programs based on scientific research that:

~ Employs systematic, empirical methods that draw on observation or experiment.

~ Involves rigorous data analyses that are adequate to test the stated hypotheses and justify the general conclusions drawn.

~ Relies on measurements or observational methods that provide valid data across evaluators and observers and across multiple measurements and observations.

~ Has been accepted by a peer-reviewed journal or approved by a panel of independent experts through a comparably rigorous, objective and scientific review.[15] Furthermore, NCLB requires that these five essential components be included in the reading program:

Phonemic Awareness

The ability to hear, identify and manipulate the individual sounds, or phonemes, in spoken words.

Phonics

The understanding that there is a predictable relationship between phonemes and graphemes, which are the letters and spelling that represents spoken language sounds.

Vocabulary Development

Development of stored information about the meanings and pronunciation of words necessary for communications.

Reading Fluency

The ability to read text accurately and quickly, providing a bridge between word recognition and comprehension. Fluent readers recognize words and comprehend at the same time.

Reading Comprehension Strategies

Strategies for understanding, remembering, and communicating with others about what has been read.[16]

We have seldom seen such detailed prescriptions placed upon public education by the government. It remains to be seen if the courts will continue their traditional deference to educators in academic matters or will enforce legislative mandates like these in NCLB.

One silver lining in the cloud of financial difficulties currently surrounding schools may be the necessity of more critical appraisal of materials before purchase. A commendable plank in platforms of many teacher groups is for a louder voice for classroom teachers in decisions about materials. When teachers address these matters, it's essential they ask how well the materials have been demonstrated to accomplish specific educational goals, and that comments on the "attractiveness of illustrations," etc., be kept in proper perspective. We must also be prepared for the fact that as we become more data-oriented in materials evaluation, some of our pet notions about materials may be shown false. For example, some evidence suggests that in early reading materials, better reading results when the illustrations are not on the same page as the text. Many teachers, while observing an occasional child who "reads" the pictures rather than the words, still believe that illustrations add enough interest to belong with the text. Time will tell.

Selection of Materials to Meet Specific Objectives

Imagine a third grade teacher with 22 children, three reading at a 7th grade level and five not reading at all. Suppose the teacher could push a button and receive full information on materials appropriate for those children as well as the boy with a severe spelling problem and the gifted girl interested in science. This can be done now through a variety of approaches where materials are classified on several dimensions including reading level required, interest level, mode of presentation, individual or group use and so on. However, there are limitations both in their lack of availability to teachers and in teacher dependence on the accuracy and completeness of information fed into the system.

A process which might be best described as backwards is often involved in materials selection. We recently observed this in miniature at a convention exhibit of a new program for primary grades. This program came neatly packaged in a large box, had accompanying workbooks, and featured a puppet-like character. A teacher was overheard to say, "Oh, isn't that cute? My children would really like this. I think I'll order it. I wonder what it does?" The decision to order was followed by the almost incidental question of the purpose of the materials. A very different situation would exist if a list were available of specific objectives to be attained by students in every classroom. We would start with an objective such as, "Correctly solve 19 of 20 problems using the concept of 'equals' in the process of counting to the same number on both sides of the equal sign," and then ask whether the material under consideration would assist children in reaching that goal.

Presently it's possible to sell materials regardless of the presence of specific goals. An editorial staff party was held in the offices of a publisher well known for auditory and visual perception training programs. As a gag, one of the editors prepared a prospectus for a "new" program called POT (Perceptual Olfactory Training). The prospectus outlined, in biting satire of professional jargonese, the rationale for the importance of improved olfactory senses complete with diagrams of the nose. Training activities were suggested for the classroom and a special smelling board provided with garlic, perfume, etc. Even as the group chuckled appreciatively, it was frighteningly clear to all that the "POT Program" could be presented to the educational world and be taken seriously by some. The possibility exists that some programs on the market could have had similar origins.

Few teachers today have time to construct their own educational materials when none can be located or afforded which meet the planned objectives. However, paraprofessionals can and do perform many materials preparation services. Some of our states and larger districts provide systematic aid to teachers in preparing and producing classroom materials. Hopefully, this trend will accelerate.

Teacher Evaluation of Materials

Systems need to be implemented in each classroom with the teacher obtaining exact information on student performances with materials. Knowing how effective materials are in one's classroom is just as important as data on how students in a different section of the country performed seven years ago.

Tutors, Aides and Volunteers

Most new teachers — general and special education — now receive training in team teaching, collaborative teaching, consultations. Rare is the teacher who doesn't function also on an IEP team or as a member of a student study team or other similar group.

However, teachers do not always receive as much training in working with tutors, aides and volunteers who have varying degrees of professional training. The overriding principle in all these working relationships should be the best interest of the child, and require that student interest needs be embedded in a win-win relationship between involved adults.

The key to maintaining a smooth relationship between the teacher and other adults is a clear understanding of their respective roles. A factor that must be considered is the relative expertise of teacher to other adult. The usual presumption is that the teacher has the greater expertise and should be the leader.

Another important factor is legal, i.e., by law certain classroom functions must be performed or supervised by a certified person. Those boundaries should be clear to all from the outset.

The Well-Qualified Private Tutor

This tutor can pose somewhat of a difficulty for some teachers. Often the family of a special education student has contracted with a private tutor who has special expertise in a particular methodology, such as Orton-Gillingham reading, Alphabetic Phonics, Wilson Reading, Discrete Trials Training (DTT), Sensory Integration, etc. The parents have become convinced that a particular methodology or practitioner will benefit their child more than the program offered by the school district and, as allowed under IDEA, they seek reimbursement from the district.

Fortunately, this situation does not occur very often. However, when it does, it can be troublesome. It frequently happens that the hiring of the tutor is the first step in what becomes a legal action, such as a due process hearing, against the district. In a hearing, questions and charges fly. Why didn't the teacher use the method or program at issue? Why did the child (allegedly) make more progress with the tutor than with the teacher? Did the teacher know the child needed the tutor's expertise? When the tutored student is a general education student, the parents may request the teacher to make changes in how she deals with the student to accomodate the wishes or beliefs of the tutor or the family.

There is no one answer as to how these issues should be handled, except to say that cooperative, professional relationships, focused on the child, will help solve the problems.

Evaluation

Chapter V

The ultimate evaluation of the educative process, including that portion conducted by schools, will be whether humankind survives. If we survive overpopulation, environmental degradation, and a propensity for violence, the next evaluative question will be the quality of our survival. To answer this, we must return to a question raised early in our discussion. Of what benefit are literacy skills if they are not employed toward positive goals? With even our existence perhaps in jeopardy, does it make sense to evaluate education in terms of achievement in academic areas? Of course it does, but not if they are the only measures of how well the school is performing.

The heart of evaluation lies in the first step of teaching — in formulating objectives. If objectives are clearly constructed, meaningful evaluation is possible, though sometimes difficult. If objectives are not clear, evaluation is ambiguous, subjective and less-than-satisfactory. Suppose that one objective of a newly instituted secondary counseling program were to reduce the drop-out rate in the junior class from a current rate of 35% to 10% within the first two years of the program. It would be relatively simple to determine whether the drop-out rate had been reduced to that level. Attributing the reduction to the counseling program would be somewhat more complex. But if the drop-out rate were reduced to 7% and it seemed reasonable to credit the counseling program with a part of the reduction, most of us would feel the objective had been met. If, on the other hand, the objectives of the new program had been to "provide guidance to assist each student to reach his or her maximum potential for social, vocational and academic development" no true evaluation would be possible. The supporters of the program might cite that 15% of the students in the high school voluntarily talked to the counselors about matters of concern to them, while critics could argue that grades of students seen by counselors didn't improve and drug abuse had increased during the two years. The volley would likely go on and on.

In a state which did not yet have public kindergartens, one large district attempted to sell the taxpayers on supporting a local kindergarten program. One proposal was to start a small demonstration kindergarten which (hopefully) would be so successful taxpayers would see the benefits of expanding it for all five-year-olds in the district.

But what constitutes success in a kindergarten program? Suppose the stated objectives of the kindergarten were "to provide an individualized program which meets the social, emotional, and cognitive needs of each child?" How could taxpayers be persuaded that it had accomplished this and therefore should be expanded? On the other hand, suppose a major objective was to, "Reduce to less than 1% the rate of retention by teaching children in the kindergarten program to perform these tasks":

1. Count to 20 with no help and to 100 with help at the decades.

2. Print own first and last name legibly.

3. Identify 10 common colors by name.

4. Correctly match and name these geometric shapes — circle, square, triangle, rectangle.

5. Correctly follow verbal directions to draw lines over, under, between, and around pictured objects.

With objectives spelled out this clearly, it would be easy for a district to objectively and accurately communicate to the taxpayers the extent to which the kindergarten program was achieving the desired objectives.

Another value which inheres in the use of specific objectives is that they tend to create a positive self-fulfilling prophecy. When we have a clear goal, we expect to reach it, and that expectancy seems to combine with the direction and sense of purposefulness provided by the goal. Having formulated the objective increases the chance of reaching it.

Knowledge of progress made toward explicit goals — particularly short term ones — powerfully enhances self-esteem and feelings of competency for teacher and student. Sequential ladders of specific objectives already accomplished, as well as those yet to be reached, provide visible reminders of our ability to achieve. The more we do and know we have done, the more we can do in the future.

The most serious hindrance to evaluations which enable us to make rational, data-based decisions about education is the lack of written objectives specified in terms of measurement strategies. The urgency of the need for school administration at every level to formulate and candidly explicate the educational objectives of states, districts, buildings, grade levels, research projects, and experimental programs cannot be overstated. This must be followed by equally candid evaluation of the school's success in meeting these objectives.

Many educators recall the debates created when certain state departments of education determined that reading achievement scores would be published in local newspapers. The taxpayers were to know how the reading scores of the children in their communities compared to those in other communities and how they fared according to national norms. The issues were often confounded by political and personality factors; nevertheless, many educators were enraged that their efforts, as reflected in student test scores, should be held up to the scrutiny of the citizens who pay their salaries. The educators' protests ranged far and wide: Such data cannot be properly interpreted by mere citizens; tests were unfair because they tested general reading and were not limited to the vocabulary contained in state-adopted programs; individual state data handling and compilation were not above question; low scores were due to migrant and other diverse groups, but would be interpreted as the fault of the schools; districts should not be compared with each other because they vary widely on many social and cultural dimensions; parents would be unduly harsh with school personnel and budgets in areas where scores were low; a short school day was at fault, not the reading instruction; ad infinitum.

These objections and others may have been valid, invalid or partially valid. Regardless, NCLB now requires that assessment results be available to the public in the form of report cards on student achievement.

Yearly States and School District Must Publicly Report:

~ Information on student achievement at each proficiency level on the state academic assessment, categorized by race, ethnicity, gender, disability status, migrant status, English proficiency, and status as economically disadvantaged (except in a case in which the number of students in a category is insufficient to yield statistically reliable information or the results would reveal personally identifiable information about an individual student).

~ A comparison between the actual academic achievement levels of each group of students and the state's annual measurable objectives for each group of students.

~ The percentage of students in each category.

~ The most recent two-year trend in student achievement in each academic area, and for each grade level (for which assessments are required by NCLB).

~ Graduation rates for secondary school students.

~ The performance of districts regarding making adequate yearly progress, including the name of each school identified for school improvement.

~ The professional qualifications of teachers in the state, the percentage of instructors teaching with emergency or provisional credentials, and the percentage of classes in the state not taught by highly qualified teachers, in all schools and in high-poverty compared to low-poverty schools.[1]

The impression emerged in years past that many educators opposed an open and public evaluation of reading instruction. Now, the trend toward accountability has resulted in mandated evaluation of our schools. NCLB requires that each state develop a single, statewide accountability system with assessments that measure how well students master state-developed content standards. By 2003, states must have content standards in math and reading/language arts in grades 3 – 8. By 2005-2006, content standards must be in place for science, covering grade spans 3 – 5, 6 – 9 and 10–12.

The actual assessment of student performance begins in 2004-2005 when states must administer tests in math and reading/language arts in grades 3 – 5, 5 – 9, and 10–12. Science testing begins no later than 2007-2008.

Many states have also developed or are developing extensive "high-stakes" testing used as the basis for promotion and graduation. Concern has developed in some quarters — concern that mandated testing will result in teaching to the tests at the expense of other aspects of the educational program. To look at this issue thoughtfully, we need to back up. What was the impetus for high-stakes testing and NCLB in the first place? The public schools of the nation were not doing a satisfactory job of teaching basic skills and science, whether measured by comparison with other countries or by society's expectations.

If one effect of the tests is to focus more teaching time and effort on reading, language arts, math and science, that would seem to be in line with the intent of the testing. This emphasis might be at the expense of some other program offerings, but that, too, would seem to reflect the intent. It is not unreasonable to believe there is a positive correlation between time spent in teaching a content subject and student achievement in that area. Another approach would be to lengthen the school day, week or year. However, budget crises faced in some states are forcing shortened hours, not added school time.

A related concern is that by "teaching to the test," instructors may teach only factual specifics, losing the big picture and perhaps missing out on spontaneous, incidental, "teachable" moments that happen in classrooms. This possibility presumes that teachers have access to the tests, a highly unlikely occurrence. Teachers may correctly assume that a sixth grade math test will have items requiring division of fractions and conversion of decimals to fractions and vice versa. Such skills are on the tests because they are in the curriculum. Tests do not create a new curriculum; they reflect the curriculum.

Tests reflect the curriculum in at least two different ways. Standardized tests sample the curriculum, and scores on the sample are compared to scores of other students. If a student knows the sampled bits, which appear on the test, she probably knows the other bits, too. If in fact a teacher were to know ahead of time exactly which sampled "bits" were to be on a standardized test and taught just those bits, the critics' worst fears would be realized. This possibility, however unlikely, must be guarded against.

Some teachers feel a good deal of pressure to have their students perform well on these tests. This is understandable. Much is at stake, for the student, family, teacher and school.

The types of program assessment and evaluation at a state and district level may prove to be valuable as well as controversial. Our major focus, however, is on teaching, so let us now look at educational evaluation from the classroom teacher's view. Some classroom evaluation is related to a final, end-of-year "summing up." How well did my teaching go this year with this group of students? How well did they perform on the end-of-year national or state achievement tests? How many are achieving substantially below grade level?

But evaluation is also related to day-by-day decision making. Is this child ready to be moved to a different reading group? Is this high-interest, low-vocabulary series the best one to use with Jacob? Is Ashley ready for the rest of the multiplication tables or should she practice the fives and sixes another day?

Is it better for this group to have the spelling test on Wednesday with free days for those who get all the words right or on Friday and provide more practice for all children first? Do the students need more practice in arithmetic computation? Are they bored because the social studies material is too easy or frustrated because it is beyond them? Is their error rate going up in spelling or does it just seem that way?

The end-of-year process is called summative evaluation and the day-by-day decision- making kind is formative evaluation. Both are important but serve different purposes.

Summative evaluation describes the final product — how it turned out. Formative evaluation tells the teacher how it is going at the time and provides the basis for rational decisions about when a change in teaching techniques, in materials, seating arrangement or class schedule needs to be made so that more effective and efficient learning can take place.

Summative Evaluation

Standardized tests are not the only form of summative evaluation in education, but they are the most frequently used. Other end-of-year summing up measures would include average daily attendance, dropout totals, and so on.

Characteristics of standardized tests

Standardization is the process of administering a test to a large sample of children selected according to predetermined characteristics such as age, locale and IQ. The performance of this normative group of children then becomes the norm against which other children's scores are compared. These scores are most often expressed in grade levels, percentiles (or stanines or deciles) and standard scores. These normative referenced scores share one characteristic — the individual child's performance is compared to that of other children. If no other children had previously taken such a test, it would not be possible to describe given student's performance as a 2.7 grade level, a standard score of 83, or a 40th percentile.

Another important characteristic of standardized tests is that they are designed to sample bits of knowledge which represent the subject's knowledge of a broad area. In a test of musical composers and compositions, if one has adequate knowledge in this field, he could identify many composers and compositions, making particular ones included on the test of little consequence. In some areas, such as elementary arithmetic, problems can arise from this approach. Suppose, for example, that the test includes a heavy smattering of new mathematics and is administered to children who have been taught only traditional mathematics, or suppose column formats for addition and subtraction appear on a test administered to children who have had only linear formats. Problems in assessing reading occur when a child with carefully programmed reading instruction (which dealt with phonically regular words) is given a test derived from readers weighted with irregular sight words such as one, laugh or city.

Use of Standardized Tests

Teachers must be alert to the possible "unfair" uses of scores from standardized tests under circumstances like those described. Remember, norms don't lie — that is not the problem. In the group on whom the test was standardized, the average child in the 6th month of 2nd grade scored 40 words correct. But if your students at the same point in 2nd grade score only 10 words right, the problem could have been that the test was on something your students weren't expected to know and it failed to test what they had been taught. In these cases where teachers recognize a test is inappropriate (either because the students differ from the standardization group or because it doesn't adequately sample or represent what they have been taught), supplemental testing should be sought. These might well be criterion tests based on the skills ladders which have been taught.

For years it has been said one must not "teach to the test." This is because it's the intention of many tests to sample a few specifics which represent an area. When a test is designed to do this and is standardized on students who have been taught more broadly, then teaching answers to specific questions is inconsistent with fair play. But just the opposite applies to criterion-referenced tests where the test item IS the desired behavior. Here, an entirely different principle applies: If it's worth testing, it's worth teaching. If the desired performance and the criterion test item are to write the numerals 1 to 9 legibly in 10 seconds, then that is what should be taught and practiced. If a child is to be tested for rote recall of the multiplication tables, she should be taught to recall them by rote.

Many schools use computer scoring and reporting of standardized test scores. More useful to teachers and curriculum staff than summaries by grade, etc., are item analyses in which the numbers of children passing each item are noted. Teachers could examine the specific items on which significant numbers of children are having difficulty and see if they reveal any changes which need to be made in teaching or in content. This is a judgmental matter in which educators must determine whether an item or group of items represents an important area. If the children are failing on these vital areas, then the standardized test has produced valuable data for educational decision-making.

Student achievement test scores, as well as a multitude of other factors, may enter into debates on the fairness of merit pay or other efforts to reward teacher competency. But, using standardized test data for these purposes remains extremely problematic. When NCLB-mandated "report cards" on school performance becomes widely attended to, we may see unexpected ramifications of publicizing evaluation data.

Formative Evaluation

A task ladder containing objectives and sub-objectives provides a meaningful way for the teacher to track pupil progress in many areas. An individual child can be described in terms of his status on any task ladder. Data can also be easily compiled for children on any ladder.

Two Advantages of a Task Ladder-Based Evaluation:

~ it's precise and true, describing a child's status fairly and behaviorally, and

~ it provides an ever-present guide to the teacher regarding what to teach next.

Disadvantages Include:

~ the expectations of others for more general and global kinds of evaluation such as those provided by an IQ, a letter grade or an achievement test score,

~ it provides information only about what to teach next, but not how to teach it,

~ it provides only crude data on the efficiency with which the teaching of any task was accomplished, and

~ it gives no information on how different children responded to teaching techniques.

For example, two children may both be able to perform the same task, but at different speeds. If Alvin read the story in 10 minutes and answered all the comprehension questions correctly, would his reading ability be accurately described the same as Benny's who needed 35 minutes to read the same story and also answered the questions? What about a comparison of the student who always finishes his arithmetic first with no errors and his buddy who never finishes without using recess time, but also does careful and accurate work? Is the speed with which work is accomplished a factor teachers need to weigh in making educational decisions? Do we have any systematic way for teachers to obtain data on speed of children's performance?

Accuracy is a more visible variable than speed for the simple reason that when an answer is inaccurate, it is wrong! But, how do we systematically observe change in the degree of accuracy in a child's work? Remember the child who miscalled every other word? How did his accuracy in reading Cowboy Sam compare to that he achieved when he was switched to the Underwater Adventure series? How did class accuracy change over the course of the long division problems presented for practice? These kinds of questions can be answered by most teachers in general terms. Would more precise information be helpful in deciding which reading books to use at a given stage in reading instruction, or how many long division problems should be given and when? There is a system that provides this information, for each child and for the total classroom, and which avoids having to rely on trial and error.

Precision Teaching

Precision teaching is an evaluation system developed by Lindsley and extended by Haughton, Kunzelmann, and others.[2, 3]

Procedures of Precision Teaching:

1. Pinpoint the behavior to be changed, so it is a countable movement cycle (behavior), such as digits written, words read orally, or words written in response to a story starter.

2. Record the rate (per minute) at which the behavior is presently occurring. Time during which the behavior is counted may vary from all day to a minute or less. Rate is recorded on six-cycle logarithmic paper.[4]

3. Change something (the events which follow the behavior or the stimuli preceding it) to increase or decrease the behavior, as appropriate.

4. Evaluate the effect of the change on the behavior chart and if necessary, try a different change.

The four steps of precision teaching closely resemble the four essential teacher behaviors outlined in this book. Pinpointing behavior to be changed corresponds to writing objectives behaviorally. Examples of targeted movement cycles to be accelerated or decelerated are: Words read orally, letters written legibly, hand raises, smiles, — they can be observed and counted. Corresponding behavioral objectives might be "read words orally at 80 per minute with 2 or fewer errors," or "write legible letters at 100 per minute." In pinpointing behaviors to be changed and in formulating objectives, the person whose behavior is being changed can specify the behavior and the objective, or this can be done cooperatively between teacher and pupil. In many academic areas we now have data on acceptable rates (see discussion of fluency in preceding chapter). If a child is unduly slow in doing arithmetic problems or in copying work from the chalkboard, we must determine what constitutes an appropriate target rate. How fast do students who are working at a "average" rate do simple subtraction problems? With precision teaching, the teacher can take a one-minute time sample on the entire class and readily determine the range of rates at which the children are now operating. Error rates can be obtained at the same time as rates correct.

Recording rate provides the means to view students daily learning. The chart with its daily rate recordings allows the teacher and student to plan instruction. This corresponds loosely to analyzing tasks. The charts provide precise information about whether the child is learning the subskills, i.e., whether they are being taught adequately for the child. If an entire group of students showed in their charts that their performance was not improving rapidly enough, it might be that the task analysis was inadequate.

First and second grade students have been taught to do their own charting, which often proves an incentive to better work. If, however, time samples of other than one minute are used, division or conversion is necessary to chart rate per minute. For this reason some primary teachers use one-minute timed samples almost exclusively. For oral reading, arithmetic, writing, and many other areas this seems quite adequate. Kunzelmann[5] has developed an aid called the "Countoon." The Countoon can be kept at the student's desk to help him do the counting. The teacher can then convert to rates and chart the data. The following is an adapted example of a Countoon depicting the pinpointed behavior to be changed, the child's count, and the consequences. For each five occasions the child raises his hand before speaking, he gets to help the teacher pass out papers to the class.

WHAT I DO	MY COUNT	WHAT HAPPENS
	1 2 3 4 5 6 7 8 9 10 11 12 13 14 15 16 17 18 19 20	5 =

"countoon"

The charts reveal when something in the educational setting needs to be changed. If an undesired behavior or an error rate is holding its own or accelerating, something must be done differently. Similarly, if a desired or correct rate is failing to increase, change is needed. Nothing within the precision teaching system itself dictates what to change, although experience with changing the difficulty of the material, studying conditions, or consequences used builds up quickly and teachers develop favorite successful change tactics. Charts quickly show if the selected change is effective for this child. For example, let's say our experience with arithmetic dawdlers has been consistently successful when we introduced free time as a reward for increases in rate of solving problems correctly. Free time may have dramatically helped 30 children become more proficient in arithmetic computation, and yet be totally ineffective with the 31st child. The daily rates will reveal this to the teacher and indicate clearly that free time should be replaced by something else. Again, the chart does not say what to try — this must come from the teacher's good judgment, experience, prior data or hunch. It will enable the teacher and student to see within days whether the new choice of intervention is working. The act of "changing something" is directly comparable to our third cluster of behaviors — teaching. Some practitioners of precision teaching and other behaviorally-based educational strategies focus on changing the consequences of the behavior; on insuring that completion of the task produces something satisfying and worthwhile to the child (stars, M & M's, free time, special privileges, new problems). We have no quarrel with the teacher insuring consequences are effective. In fact, we insist on this. Sometimes, however, what children need is not louder praise or more points, but better teaching. Most of us could not improve our performance on a test in nuclear physics no matter how we're rewarded for it unless we were taught concepts previously unknown to us. If we put the student response in the center of the educational event, where it properly belongs, we see that any teaching-learning situation can be described in this simple form showing "before," "behavior," and "after" *(See Table 1)*.

Table 1:
Before, Student's Behavior, and After

Before (Antecedents) All the conditions, materials, teaching behaviors relevant to the child's making the response.	**Student's Behavior** The pinpointed behavior to be increased or decreased.	**After** (Consequences) The "what happens" as a result of the occurrence of the behavior.
Reader level II.	Words correctly read orally in one minute.	Every 10 words = 1 point 10 points = 1 minute free time.
Standing at the chalkboard.	Hits another child.	Every hit = loss of 10 minutes of recess.
Teacher dictating spelling words.	Words spelled correctly.	Each word = 1¢ play money to be spent at room store.
Seated at front of room.	Raises hand before talking.	Each day with 100% = 1 turn to carry message to office.

The "after" column depicts consequences often emphasized by behaviorally-oriented educators. When the behavior to be changed is social or non-academic, such as initiating friendly conversation with peers or decreasing self-put-downs like "I can't do it," results are often obtained by changing consequences. However, when the behavior to be changed is academic, the teacher must first establish that the student can perform the task; i.e., decode new words, borrow when subtracting. Then changing the consequences will help. If the child is unable to perform, make changes in the "before" column; use a different reading book, present a new concept, reteach, lecture. Precision teaching tells us how effective our educational decision was — it does not tell us which decision to make or what instructional technique to try. It's an evaluation, not an intervention tool.

The advantages of using data like these in the classroom are many. Most important, it allows the teacher to see the daily results of teaching and to know when changes are needed. It provides a systematic opportunity for children to be involved in pinpointing academic and affective behaviors they would like to change, in deciding how to change them and in recording and evaluating their own progress toward those goals. The use of standardized charts in precision teaching means that data collected can be directly compiled and compared. Benefits to the researcher are evident. Additionally, any two or more teachers can directly compare notes on student performances, on materials, on the effectiveness of free time versus M & M's, on numbers of disruptive behaviors — on anything on which they both have gathered data. The information provided by charted rate measures on speed and accuracy of student performance, on the stimulus situation (e.g., phonic worksheets, programmed arithmetic) and on consequences allows precise determination of how these affect student responses.

Formative evaluation should help the teacher make confident and correct decisions on a daily basis. Any evaluation system which does that and is practical in terms of expense and teacher time brings about improved achievement for student and increased satisfaction for teachers. We do not advocate for any one system of formative evaluation. Rather, our extended description of precision teaching illustrates the main features of classroom formative evaluation from a teacher's point of view. Any system which yields precise and objective data about student performance will do the job.

The teacher who begins writing measurable objectives behaviorally, analyzing tasks, and evaluating outcomes more precisely, might begin experiencing more positive thoughts about the profession of teaching.

Recycle or Rejoice

Chapter VI

After the objectives have been formulated, the learning tasks analyzed, the teaching done, and the evaluation finished, it's time to recycle or rejoice. And then to move on.

More errors are probably made by moving to new material too soon than by recycling too often. Unfortunately, one result of this tendency is the failure of many students to achieve real fluency in important skills.

The more frequently evaluations are conducted, the more quickly we can catch the need for reteaching, before major gaps have developed in student learning. When rate data, discussed in the last chapter, are collected in daily one minute samples, the teacher can usually determine the effectiveness of the intervention (teaching) within seven to ten days. This is far superior to allowing weeks or even months to go by before doing an evaluation.

When evaluation reveals reteaching or further practice is necessary, it must be provided. On the other hand, when evaluation shows instruction was successful, the teacher deserves more praise and thanks than she will likely receive. Successful teaching is sometimes difficult, and always valuable.

Our message to teachers is simple and direct. We "OTTER" teach as well as we can by recognizing the importance and roles of **Objectives**, **Task analysis**, **Teaching**, **Evaluation**, and **Recycling or rejoicing**. The goal of this book has been to assist teachers in their journey to become consumate professionals whose repertoires of knowledge and skills include:

1. Specifying **objectives** behaviorally, precisely and measurably;

2. **Analyzing tasks** into essential subskills or utilizing those direct instruction programs which have already done this well;

3. **Teaching** directly, correcting appropriately, reinforcing frequently and managing behavior and the classroom efficiently and positively;

4. **Evaluating** objectively the results of teaching; and

5. **Recycling**, i.e., changing antecedents or consequences as needed, and, when the evaluation has shown the teaching to have been effective, then **rejoicing** and moving on.

Notes

Introduction

1. Perry, A.C. (1912). *The Status of the Teacher*. Boston, MA: Houghton Mifflin.

Chapter I:

1. Zigmond, N. (1997). Educating students with disabilities: The future of special education. In J. Lloyd, E. Kameenui, & D. Chard. (Eds.), *Issues in educating students with disabilities pp.* 377-390. Mahwah, N.J.: Earlbaum (p. 379).

2. Englemann, S. (1997). Theory of mastery and acceleration. In J. Lloyd, E. Kameenui, & D. Chard. (Eds.), *Issues in educating students with disabilities.* pp. 177-195. Mahwah, N.J.: Earlbaum. (p. 178).

3. Hugh Downs, WGN TV, 3/29/03.

4. Sowards, G. W. (1969). The Florida State University model program for the preparation of elementary school teachers. *Journal of Research and Development in Education, 2, 3*. Spring, 1969.

5. Goodlad, J. I. (1969). The school versus education. *Saturday Review*, April, 1969.

6. Engelmann, S. (1967). Teaching reading to children with low mental ages. 193-201. *Education and Training of the Mentally Retarded, 2* (193-4).

Chapter II:

1. Popham, W. J. (1969). Probing the validity of arguments against behavior goals. Cited in Kibler, R. J., Barker, L.L., & Miles, D.T. (1970). *Behavioral objectives and instruction*. Boston: Allyn and Bacon, Inc.

2. Gronlund, N.E. (1970). *Stating behavioral objectives for classroom instruction*. Toronto, Ontario, Canada: Macmillan.

3. Bloom, B. S., & Engelhart, M.D., Furst, E.G., Hill, W.H., & Krathwohl, D.R. (1956). *Taxonomy of education objectives, handbook I: Cognitive domain*. New York: David McKay.

4. For a book length treatment, see Bateman, B., & Herr, C. (2003). *Writing Measurable IEP Goals and Objectives*. Verona, WI: Attainment.

5. Mager, R. F. (1962). *Preparing instructional objectives*. Palo Alto, CA: Fearon.

Chapter III:

1. For a thorough, scholarly ground-breaking treatment of designing instruction for teaching verbal associations (facts, chains, discrimination), concepts and role relationships, reading decoding, reading comprehension, mathematics (facts, concepts, operations) and expressive writing, see Kameenui, E., & Simmons, D. (1990). *Designing Instructional Strategies*. Columbia, OH: Merrill.

2. For a discussion of task "ladders" (sequential steps) and "pies" (non-sequential steps), see Bateman, B., & Herr, C. (2003). *Writing Measurable IEP Goals and Objectives*. Verona, WI: Attainment.

3. Kameenui, E., & Simmons, D. (1990). *Designing Instructional Strategies*. Columbia, OH: Merrill. (p. 433).

4. Gersten, R. (1985). Direct instruction and special education students: A review of evaluation research. *Journal of Special Education, 19,* 41-50.

5. Gersten, R., Woodward, J., & Carnine, D.W. (1987). Direct instruction research: The third decade. *Remedial and Special Education, 8*(6), 48-56.

6. Gersten, R., Woodward, J., & Darch, C. (1986). Direct instruction: A research-based approach to curriculum design and teaching. *Exceptional Children, 53,* 17-31.

7. Brophy, J., & Good, T. L. (1986). Teacher behavior and student achievement. In M. Wittrock (Ed.), *Third handbook of research on teaching* (pp: 328-375). Chicago: Rand McNally.

Chapter IV:

1. Becker, W., Engelmann, S., & Thomas. D. (1971). *Teaching: A course in applied psychology*. Chicago: Science Research Associates.

2. Adams, G.L., & Engelmann, S. (1996). Research on Direct Instruction: *25 years beyond DISTAR*. Seattle, WA: Education Achievement Systems.

3. Grossen, B. (1997). *The research base for Corrective Reading.* DeSoto, TX: SRA/McGraw-Hill.

4. Carnine, D. W., Silbert, J., & Kameenui, E. J. (1997). (1997). *Direct instruction reading* (3rd ed.). Upper Saddle River, NJ: Prentice-Hall.

5. Becker, W., Engelmann, S., & Thomas. D. (1971). Teaching: *A course in applied psychology.* Chicago: Science Research Associates.

6. See, e.g., Bateman, B. D., & Golly, A. (2003). *Why Johnny Doesn't Behave: Twenty Tips and Measurable BIPS.* Verona, WI: Attainment.

7. E.g., go to Binder Riha Associates, *www.binder-riha.com*, and Haughton Learning Center, *www.napanet.net/-hlcenter.*

8. Lindsley, O.E. (1996). Is fluency free-operant response-response chaining? *The Behavior Analyst*, 19, 211-224.

9. Haughton, E. C. (1972). Aims: Growing and Sharing. In J.B. Jordon & L.S. Robbins (Eds.), *Let's try doing something else kind of thing* (p. 20-39). Arlington, VA: Council for Exceptional Children.

10. Starlin, C. M. (1971). Evaluating progress toward reading proficiency. In B. Bateman (Ed.), *Learning Disorders, Vol IV* (p. 389-465).

11. Binder, C., Haughton, E., & Van Eyk, D. (1990). Increasing endurance by building fluency: Precision Teaching attention span. *TEACHING Exceptional Children, 22*(3), 24-27.

12. Hasselbring, T.S., et al. (1987). Developing automaticity — Special focus effective mathematics instruction. *TEACHING Exceptional Children, 19*(4), 30-33.

13. National Reading Panel. (2000). *Teaching children to read: An evidence-based assessment of scientific research literature on reading and its implications for reading instruction. Reports of the subgroups* (NIH Publication No. 00-4754). Washington, DC: U.S. Government Printing Office.

14. Chall, J.S. (1967). *Learning to read: The great debate.* New York: McGraw-Hill.

15. 20 USC 70 § 1208(6)

16. 20 USC 70 § 1208(3)

Chapter V:

1. 20 USC 70 § 1111(h)(l)

2. Haughton, E. (1969). *Counting together: Precision teaching rationale-69.* Eugene, OR; Instructional materials Center, University of Oregon.

3. Kunzelman, H. P., et al. (1970). *Precision teaching: An inital training sequence.* Seattle,WA: Special Child Publications.

4. One of the disingishing features of precision teaching is the use of six-cycle, logarithmic charts on which behavior rates of zero to 1,000 per minute can be recorded. A huge advantage of these 6-cycle charts is that change is shown multiplicably, i.e., the slope of the line showing a two-fold change from twice a minute to four times a minute is the same as the slope of the change line from 200 to 400 times a minute. As valuable and recommended as this 6-cycle chart is, we would rather see teachers use any graph paper they choose rather than not recording rate data at all.

5. Kunzelman, H. P., et al. (1970).